P.A.C.E.

PREPARE, ACT, CARE, EVACUATE.

ACTIVE SHOOTER WORKPLACE VIOLENCE
PREPAREDNESS

JAMES CAMERON, CPP

P.A.C.E./ James Cameron, CCP. —1st ed.

Paperback: 978-1-5323-9601-4

eBook: 978-1-5323-9602-1

Contents

About the Author

James Cameron is an ASIS International Board-Certified Protection Professional, CPP, and has over fifteen years of international security experience. He is a member of the ASIS Executive Protection Council and has operated Security Concepts Group since 2009. Mr. Cameron is a combat veteran, having served as an Army Ranger under the Special Operations Command during his enlistment. Mr. Cameron also has earned his Bachelor's Degree in Business Information Systems.

Mr. Cameron has worked with the U.S. State Department as a member of the Diplomatic Security Services. There, he served in multiple positions, including Security Detail Leader for the U.S. Ambassador to Iraq and Afghanistan. He ultimately finished as an instructor and subject matter expert for the High Threat, Dignitary Protection Division of the U.S. Department of State Diplomatic Security Services.

Mr. Cameron's experience spans the globe, ranging from providing protection under hostile fire in non-permissive, high-threat environments, to providing first responder medical care during multiple mass casualty situations in Iraq, Afghanistan, and Chad. Additionally, Mr. Cameron has travelled around the world teaching Non-Governmental Organizations (NGOs) techniques on the avoidance of harm to personnel assigned to permissive, semi-permissive, and non-permissive environments.

Mr. Cameron's experience led him to Dubai, where he worked directly for the Royal family as head security liaison in charge of the Sheikh's personal protection. Mr. Cameron's responsibilities also included all training of security personnel, advance travel coordination, and the security of international VIP visitors.

Since Mr. Cameron opened Security Concepts Group for business in 2009, he has raised the standards of protection, including implementing multiple added value benefits that others now try to imitate. Under Mr. Cameron's leadership, experience, and vision, Security Concepts Group has grown from providing only Close Personal Protection to now offering a wide range of security solution services to include, the first of its kind, Active Assailant/Workplace Violence Preparedness Program.

Preface

Thank you for taking a moment to pick up this very important book on Workplace Violence, and Active Assailant prevention and preparedness. Sadly, over the years, we have seen an increase in mass casualty situations and it's only getting worse. Without a doubt, by the time you are reading this book, many more workplace violence and Active Assailant situations have occurred.

To give some background on why I am writing this book, it all started December 2, 2015, when a husband and wife, Syed Rizwan Farook, and Tashfeen Malik (female), armed with two rifles, two handguns, and an explosive device, began shooting in the parking lot of the inland regional center in San Bernardino, California. They moved inside the building, shooting at the coworkers of one of the shooters. Fourteen people were killed; twenty-two were wounded. The shooters fled the scene, but they were killed a few hours later during an exchange of gunfire with law enforcement.

This situation made me look into what training was out there for organizations and individuals besides Run-Hide-Fight. To me, Run-Hide-Fight is a one-dimensional way to approach the topic of Workplace Violence or Active Assailant (formerly known as Active Shooter).

I found at that time that no real effective training existed. This is why I developed the P.A.C.E. (Prepare-Action-Care-Evacuate) program. My unique P.A.C.E. program helped to deal with topics never before addressed during these situational training. Even now, three years later, with multiple incidents causing hundreds of deaths and even more casualties, there is no real effective training that can compare to this program.

Most—if not all—training books, classes, and seminars only discuss how to survive once you are already in an Active Assailant type attack. What if we could prepare ahead of time? How can we be prepared ahead of time? Could this preparedness possibly prevent us from even being in the situation in the first place? I'm not so arrogant to say that, yes, by reading this book you will no longer have to worry about being in an Active Assailant situation; however, what I am saying is you will be better prepared in the event that you are.

What you will find within the pages of this book are real life examples of situations that I personally have been involved in. You will also find answers to questions you didn't know you had. I will also pose questions that only you can answer since every person and organization is different. This book isn't written based on attending a few seminars, or doing some online training; rather, it is based on real life and real lessons learned.

I will dive deep into how to prepare for an incident with the hope that one never occurs. We will examine what critical actions beyond Run-Hide-Fight need to be taken during an incident. One such topic I will discuss in detail, is how to provide emergency medical care to the wounded that could save lives. This is one of the most important chapters that sets us apart from all other books on the topic of Active Assailant. When it comes to medical care, every second counts to the wounded in an Active Assailant attack, and I have seen that first hand.

The threat is forever evolving and so are the tactics, techniques, and procedures (TTPs). This book is written to be a foundation that each person and organization can use. The topics and recommendations covered in this book are solid building blocks that won't change in their importance.

The overall goal is to be prepared, have the right mindset, and know what you need to do to survive what could be the worst day of your life.

How to use this book

This book is based on a complete training program; initially, it should be read in chapter order. After that, it's best to think of it as reference material. Highlighting certain text, verses, and chapters to insure key points are remembered.

This training has been used as a base for organizational policy and procedures so keep that in mind when reading this book. Instead of thinking of this book as a book, think of it as a manual or a "Workplace Violence, Active Assailant Prevention and Preparedness for Dummies." Once read completely, this book should be referenced with respects to Workplace Violence and Active Assailant policy, procedures, and training.

Lessons Learned

Live as if you were to die tomorrow. Learn as if you were to live forever –
Mahatma Gandhi

Most training and books in this category begin with a bunch
of statistics of mass causality situations. I think we can all
agree that those situations occur way too often and way too
many are injured, or worse, killed. It is important to know
that Active Assailant attacks occur with no discernable pattern of location, weapon type, ideology, or duration of the attack. Although it may appear based on media coverage that
attacks primarily take place in one type of location over another, this is not true. The one constant statistic is that the individual or individuals expressed concerning communication
in one form or another prior to an attack—I will discuss this
further in the Prepare section of this book. As I mentioned in
the Preface, by the time you read this book, many more mass
casualty situations will have occurred, so any reference I will
make now will be outdated.

Instead of detailing what the current statistics are, I will
focus on some of the lessons learned over the past decade

as they pertain to Workplace Violence and Active Assailant attacks.

First, I will address why I utilized the term Active Assailant and not Active Shooter. As we have seen, threats can come in all shapes, sizes, gender, age, ideology, grievances, and any other reasons someone decides to conduct a mass homicide. Active Shooter implies that the threat will only use weapons that fire bullets, which is unfortunately not true. An industry standard definition of Active Assailant is: "An Active Assailant(s) is a person or group of persons actively engaged in killing or attempting to kill or cause serious bodily injury to a person or group of persons."

It's important to understand that the how and why are irrelevant to your survival. Active Assailants are creative and will use whatever means available to accomplish their mission. As we have seen, vehicles, bombs, and knives are just a few additional ways Active Assailants have come up with to cause harm and death.

Was Timothy McVeigh an Active Shooter? No, but he did kill 168 individuals while injuring an additional 680 when he bombed a federal building in Oklahoma in 1995. He was an Active Assailant—he was also a domestic terrorist.

To bring it closer to current time, in 2016, a man utilizing a vehicle rammed innocent pedestrians on the campus of Ohio State University. Once crashed, he exited his vehicle with a butcher knife and began chasing and attacking people. Was he an Active Shooter? No, but he was an Active Assailant.

Many types of weapons can be used in mass causality situations, to include vehicles, knives, explosives, aircraft, hammers, and pretty much any other instrument that can be manipulated to inflict harm or death. I could give example after example of Active Assailants, but again, we already know they exist. Understanding this concept is the first step in realizing how big the treat really is.

Now let's begin to address some of the lessons learned. I will cover these from the perspective of overall lessons learned; lessons learned by the first responders; lessons learned from those organizations and individuals involved in an incident; lessons learned regarding the attackers. Keep in mind these lessons learned are dynamic, meaning after each event, more lessons may be learned.

Overall Lessons Learned

Active Assailant incidents are often not spontaneous; instead, they are well planned out. Because they are planned out, pre-incident signs and indicators existed. Think of news coverage we have seen and how many witnesses or individuals who knew the suspect stated, "he/she was acting weird" or "I saw these social media posts but I didn't report it." Sadly, a lot of indicators get noticed but, for a variety of reasons, people choose not to report them. We will talk about mindset in the next few chapters, but this is one area that our mindset must change. It's ok to report suspicious activity and, at best, it might be nothing; at worst, you may have stopped another mass murder.

The assailant's behavior during the event is unpredictable. Generally, once they begin the shooting, they go the path of least resistance. This makes their planning almost impossible since they don't know what doors or access points will be open or unlocked. All they plan for is to get inside and start shooting; then, they move like water and flow to wherever they can gain access to that has targets for them to engage. This general rule does not apply to the assailants that are specifically targeting individuals. This could be in the case of domestic situations or where the assailants have selected persons they wish to harm or kill. During these situations, the assailants may continue to aggressively pursue their targets regardless of how hard it is to get to them.

Tactical intervention was too late. Many times, once the police are on the scene, the assailants self-terminate. Oddly, rather than continue and get into a gun fight with police, the assailant accepts that it is the end of the road for them. Because they have this mindset, they generally do not have an escape plan formulated.

Most incidents occur in a target rich environment and what is often referred to as *soft targets*. A soft target location is a place that is vulnerable to an attack, locations that generally lack a strong, or even modest, security posture such as schools, movie theaters, and places of business. This gives the attacker the ability to inflict maximum damage with little to no resistance in a short period of time.

Lessons Learned by First Responders

Like any group, first responders also have multiple lessons to be learned. One of the most critical lessons learned is that the initial reports are always wrong. Imagine the 911 dispatch trying to get accurate information to the responding officers based on ten, twenty, thirty, one-hundred different calls all at once, all from different sources. If you have ever played the telephone game, you know how hard it is to get simple information passed amongst a few people. Imagine that on steroids when it comes to Active Assailant reports.

Currently, the national standard of responding to an Active Assailant is to not wait, but to go in find and neutralize the threat. This is a newer technique, which supersedes the prior standard of waiting for a specialized response teams like SWAT or Special Weapons and Tactics teams. Generally speaking, when the police show up, they are outgunned and ill-equipped. With the new tactic of going to the threat without waiting, officers may show up with their service pistol and have to confront a gunman with a long rifle or shotgun. They may also have only their duty protective vest on, with no helmet, which may or may not stop long rifle ammunition. As we will discuss throughout this book, time is of the essence, so their speedy response—prepared or not—could save innocent lives. Because time is of the essence, they sacrifice proper equipment for time, which could ultimately save lives by putting theirs at risk.

Many officers also do not have the proper training. This is not a slight on the training they do have. However, the reality is that, with budgetary restraints and with all their other duties, their primary focus is not on dynamic building entries and room clearing. While I was in the army, one of my unit's specialty was room clearing (back then, we called it CQB, which is short for Close Quarters Battle). We trained continuously on the techniques of entering buildings and rooms. Even with all of our training, we had room to improve. It really is dishonest to believe that the police will be able to enter and clear rooms efficiently.

As of recent, we have also seen that because of poor officer selection, lack of training or equipment, officers have been hesitant to respond. We saw this during the Las Vegas massacre, where officers who were one floor below and one floor

above, did not take the appropriate action to draw fire away from the crowd and attempt to terminate the assailant.

We saw a similar response in Florida during the Parkland School shooting. The resource officer who was responsible to be present and stop an assailant also did not respond. Both situations caused additional injuries and loss of life.

Unfortunately, an individual will never know how they will or will not respond when faced with a life or death situation. This is not to say that all first responders will not place themselves in harm's way to protect the public. It does, however, highlight the importance of training and individual responsibility for their own self-survival if faced with an Active Assailant situation.

Recently, a judge ruled in Broward County—where the Parkland School shooting took place—that the sheriff's office was not legally obligated to protect and shield students in the shooting. The judge further commented that there was no constitutional obligation to protect students who were not in their custody. By the time you read this book, this ruling may be overturned or upheld. If it is upheld, I will let you use your imagination on how police may likely react during future events. This highlights the point that each person is responsible for their own survival.

Another major issue is crisis management. Once the call goes out that there is an Active Assailant or mass casualty situation, every agency responds. These agencies include, but are not limited to, local police, state police, local fire departments, paramedics, federal agencies such as FBI, and DHS. Although everyone is responding with the best intentions, it becomes confusing; communication becomes complicated, reports are inaccurate, and a clear chain of command takes time to establish.

A reoccurring issue is also the training—or lack of training—of paramedics to enter the scene. During an Active Assailant situation, law enforcement has control of the scene to include who can and who cannot enter. This has continued to jeopardize the lives of the wounded who need immediate care. Currently, there is a training course for medical first responders called Rescue Task Force; however, if fire departments and paramedics are trained, law enforcement agencies are still hesitant to allow them in to tend to the wounded.

This is highlighted during the Parkland shooting, where paramedics were told they were not allowed in to treat casualties. More will be discussed on this topic in the Care chapter.

Lessons Learned from those Organizations and Individuals Involved in an Incident

The biggest lesson to be learned is that those who are involved with a mass casualty situation believe that, "It would never happen to me." Mindset is critical when it comes to this topic. I will discuss mindset in the Prepare chapter of this book. Organizational failures that revolve around planning some of those issues, include:

- Organizations not having a plan: Often, organizations do not have plans on these topics because it's an expense and the attitude is, "it won't happen here so why have one."
- Plans are incomplete or outdated: Plans are often started but once the unqualified person starts to develop it, they quickly realize this topic is bigger than expected. A plan

doesn't need to be complicated; however, if you don't know the subject, it quickly becomes overwhelming.

- If there was a plan then leaders didn't know of the plan: If a full plan or even a partial plan has been created, it's often printed and sitting on a shelf of the person's office who created it. The plan was developed more as a "check the box" rather than a fully functional plan.

- Leaders never read the plan: Leaders often have the same opinion that the organization does, which is, "it won't happen here." With all the other duties and responsibilities that impact daily output, this plan is pushed to the back of importance. Again, checking the box, they received it but they did not read it or understand it.

- Leaders and staff never trained on the plan: If a plan is disseminated, it is a check the box action item. Rarely do leaders and staff together train on the plan. If training takes place, especially when incorporating local law enforcement first responders, staff become role players and lay on the ground, simulating being wounded. What do they actually get out of that training?

Without having or knowing the plan, leaders fail to provide effective and timely leadership simply because they do not know what their duties, roles, and responsibilities are. Because of these reasons, the system and leadership are completely overwhelmed, and failures occurs.

Organizations and individuals do not focus on the importance of specific skill training. Training that can include:

- Lifesaving medical training, this is not the typical CPR, AED, and first aid (luckily, we do cover this specific topic in this book)

- Crisis Management Planning
- Policy and Procedures training in topics, such as Workplace Violence and Active Assailant

Organizations have become reliant on training received by their local law enforcement agency, or by having employees watch videos. While these are tools, they might not be the best tools available. Utilizing local police is great, however, what benefits are the organization and staff really getting?

Most of the time, when local law enforcement conducts on site Active Assailant training, they generally discuss previous mass causality statistics and throw out catch phrases with no real detail into their meaning, such as "See Something, Say Something," be "Situationally Aware," and "Run-Hide-Fight."

They will then select staff or students to be role players and lay in various locations pretending to be injured. Now the question is, what benefits do the employees/students get out of laying on the floor being wounded? The truth is that there is no gain of knowledge for those role players. When local police conduct training, do they explain to their audience and go into detail on the following:

- Teaching how to identify potential red flags before an incident occurs? Or do they just tell you to *see something say something* with no real explanation?
- Discuss and explain the pathway to violence? Most people have never heard of this, so if you haven't heard of it, how can you be on the lookout for it? I will explain this in the Prepare chapter.
- The considerations that need to be thought of before you Run, Hide or Fight?
- The difference between *cover* and *concealment*?

- Teach the basic medical techniques that have been proven to save lives? Do they teach tourniquets, and pressure dressing, which are critical in mass casualty situations?

The reality is when law enforcement come to conduct a drill on Active Assailant, they are really training themselves on their tactics and techniques. The organizational training is secondary, if even really considered at all. When your staff are being role players, laying on the ground as training wounded, what are they really getting out of the training? The actuality is that it is more of a waste of time then actual training. That's the truth and that's the fact.

Next time law enforcement comes to your locations to train on Active Assailant, try to look at the training objectively. By the time you are done with this book, you will be able to teach those first responders a thing or two.

Lessons Learned Regarding the Attackers

After multiple studies by the FBI, US Secret Service, Homeland Security, and local law enforcement, they concluded that nine out of ten Active Assailants are suicidal. This is important to understand because it does affect how you should respond and it will affect how the police will respond. Most assailants' goal is to cause as much death and harm as possible, all the while knowing there is no escape for them. Ultimately, they either self-terminate or are killed by the armed first responders.

Regardless of how you and I may think, Active Assailants are not mentally deranged or acting in a diminished mental capacity. As we will discuss in the next section, most if not all, follow the "pathway to violence." Their actions are planned, and often rehearsed, prior to an event occurring.[1] What motivates the mass murder to commit these horrific acts? Most studies show that almost half of the assailants had some sort of grievance within the last year. Grievances can include one or more areas of stress. These areas could be workplace related, domestic issues, or other personal issues that caused the attacker to feel stressed to their breaking point. These are

Components to Motive	n	Percent*
Grievances	13	46%
Workplace	6	21%
Domestic	5	18%
Personal	2	7%
Ideological or racially-based	6	21%
Mental Health / Psychosis	4	14%
Political	1	4%
Fame	1	4%
Unknown	4	14%

* Percentages exceed 100 as one case had two motives.

_____

1 Components to motive taken from United States Secret Service report Mass Attacks in Public Spaces March 2018.

not independent of one another and it is possible that they are all interconnected. For example, say an assailant has domestic issues and their partner is leaving them for someone else. That alone is a stressor; however, could that situation then also affect their work performance, thus adding an additional stressor?

Other motivators that can influence the assailant include ideological, racial, or political beliefs, fame, and mental health issues.

Mass murder is most often the goal rather than criminal conduct, such as robbery. Sadly, with all the media coverage, each Active Assailant is trying to raise the body count and outdo the previous mass murder's numbers. This trend will continue, which means that if you find yourself in a situation, you need to understand that assailant's end goal is body counts.

During an Active Assailant attack, multiple weapons are utilized; this could include guns, knives, bombs, vehicles, and any combination of all. During multiple previous attacks, police have found explosives either at the attack site, in their vehicle, or in their residence. Some of those events are as recent as Parkland Florida, and Columbine High School where the assailants utilized both guns and explosives. It's been by sheer luck that these explosive devices did not go off and injure or kill. This will be addressed as a consideration in the Action section during the Run portion of Run-Hide-Fight.

Active Assailants' situations are generally over in less than ten minutes. This is critical, since the response time for first responders is on average four–seven minutes. We will discuss these times again and what medical considerations need to be addressed in the Care chapter.

Another major lesson learned is that assailants follow the Pathway to Violence and communicated their intentions prior to going on their killing spree. We will cover this topic in detail in the next section.

When we look at lessons learned, it's also important to understand re-sources available. We all know the internet is full of information, both good and bad. But most do not realize that there are specific online magazines that give detail instructions on how

to plan an attack and cause the most carnage during an attack. Three specific magazines include *Inspire*, *Dabiq*, and *Rumiyah*. These magazines might be a little dated by the time you are reading this book; however, their information will still be relevant, utilized, and studied by those wishing to do harm. These magazines were the first to suggest and recommend using a vehicle to run over unassuming pedestrians. The New York city driver attack, and the Ohio State University driver attack all got the idea and plans from these magazines. These magazines go into great detail on topics such as:

- Target Selection: where, when, and how to select the right venue for maximum impact.
- What firearms to use for the right affect and maximum casualties; this would include what weapons are easiest

concealable and those that will inflict the most devastation in the shortest amount of time.

- How to select and properly use a knife; what properties should the knife have and where is the optimal location to strike on a person.
- How to use a vehicle as a weapon; how to rent and utilize a vehicle to inflict maximum carnage. They also were the first to recommend this as an easy way to cause the biggest impact. Not only do they say to use a vehicle, but they also make recommendations on where to use the vehicle.
- How to build and deploy homemade bombs (this is where it is rumored that the Tsarnaev brothers, also known as the Boston Bombers, got their plans from). Detailed plans on how to create bombs using household items. This insures that the builder does not raise any red flags for authorities and would allow them to build pipe bombs and pressure cooker bombs, just to name a few.
- What the tactics of first responders are and how you can use them to your advantage. Conducting a single attack, then waiting for first responders, then conducting a second attack to inflict harm and chaos. They often use police reports, video footage, and media coverage from prior events to change up their tactics to defeat the responses by first responders. They post these lessons learned, so future attackers can be more prepared, thus extending their total attack time, which could result in more wounded and killed.

These are the newer, more detailed, and deadly versions of the Anarchist Cookbook, which was originally published in 1971. Believe it or not, in 2018 Homeland Security still referenced this book in their current Active Shooter training.

Now that we have an understanding on some basic lessons learned, what can we do to better prepare ourselves? In preparing for any mass casualty situation, there

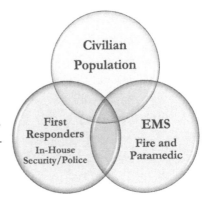

are three district roles; I call them the **Incident Preparedness Paradigm:**

- Civilian Population: Those that are directly in harm's way during an incident
- First Responders: Those can be in-house security or law enforcement
- EMS: Emergency Medical Services, those that provide critical aid to the wounded

Here are a few areas that each role can do to be better prepared:

Civilian or noncombatant population:

- Leaders should take crisis management training, which will help them develop specific plans for their location and organization. These plans can also include crisis, such as natural disasters, along with mass causality situations.
- All staff should participate either annually, semi-annually, or quarterly on workplace violence, Active Assailant prevention, and preparedness training.
- At a minimum, leaders should take additional medical training, such as bleeding control, which is currently of-

fered for free nationally, at various locations. Information on those classes can be found at bleeding control's website.[2]

- Policies and Procedures need to be developed and easy to comply with (we will discuss more on this topic in the Prepare Chapter).

- Leadership should work with local law enforcement and EMS to build relationships, which in turn create a hard target. This also gives the first responders an understanding of your organization's floorplan and layout.

- Tabletop exercises should include cross section of staff and local first responders. By having a cross section of staff, you are including additional points of view that my otherwise be missed (Definition: A tabletop exercise is an activity in which key personnel assigned emergency management roles and responsibilities are gathered to discuss, in a non-threatening environment, various simulated emergency situations).

---

2 Bleeding Control Website, http://www.bleedingcontrol.org/.

First Responders

If your organization has assigned security, either as direct hire or out-sourced, here are a few important questions they should be able to answer:

- Do security guards do more than just observe and report?

- During a Work-place Violence or Active Assailant event, what is the role of the security guard?

- If the security guard is armed, does his or her role change, and are they to engage the attacker?

- What are the security guards' rules of engagement?

- Has escalation of force been taught and authorized?

- Has de-escalation training been provided to the guard?

- Does the guard have site specific POST orders? (POST orders are written documents that clearly outline duties, responsibilities, and expectations of security guards.)

- Have they been trained to identify early warning signs and or red flags?

- Do security guards have proper training and equipment?

These questions are important because often security officers can give a sense of security. If, however, their role is not defined and these questions are not answered, all they provide is a false sense of security. Most of the time, security guards, even armed guards are Observe and Report only. This will leave employees, students, customers, clients, and bystanders exposed with no protection from security guards during an Active Assailant event.

Emergency Medical Services or EMS

- Should partake in response training, such as Rescue Task Force. This training focuses on Paramedics and Fire Rescue personnel to enter a Hot Zone, or an area where the police have not fully cleared. This allows EMS to immediately begin to treat the wounded, thus potentially saving lives.

- Advance trauma pre-hospital life support training. Specific training for mass casualty situations is critical. General training does not cover the injuries, trauma, and triage associated with a mass casualty situation.
- They should work on their community relations. By continuously working with local businesses, they are better prepared if an event was to happen. Having an understanding of building layouts, relationship

with management and employees will help in a crisis situation.

- They should be an essential part of table top training with local business key leadership and other government agencies. Their input can be critical when it comes to organizational planning. What may work on paper for management, may not work for the first responder. This is an excellent opportunity for all groups involved to discuss options and develop a plan that works for all parties involved during a crisis.

Interagency training along with private sector involvement is critical for any level of success. Taking these simple steps could be enough to warn of a potential attack based on your level of preparedness.

Prepare

If You Fail to Prepare You Are Prepared to Fail – Benjamin Franklin

The first thing anyone needs to do to be prepared is have the right mindset. Simply put, you need to understand and recognize that there is always the potential for a workplace violence situation, Active Assailant scenario, or any other type of life-threatening emergency situation. Without having this mindset, all the training in the world won't make a difference because you don't believe it could happen to you. Ironically, this is the same uttered phrase after every mass casualty situation.

In order to get started, it's important to define

a few terms that have been used and will be used throughout this book.

Workplace Violence per most recent OSHA definition:

Workplace violence is any act of threat of physical violence, harassment, intimidation, or other threatening disruptive behavior that occurs at the work site. It ranges from threat and verbal abuse to physical assaults and even homicide. It can affect and involve employers, client, customers and visitors.

Types of Workplace Violence

Various government groups to include FBI, DHS, and others have described five types of Workplace Violence. Only when workplace violence is broken down and understood can individuals prevent, report, and respond to any incidents efficiently and effectively. By understanding these five types, you will also be  better prepared to identify vulnerabilities and ultimately help mitigate the security gaps that may exist for each type.

Type One: Criminal Intent
Workplace violence that involves a criminal is usually a random act where the primary motive is theft.

More often than not, the criminal has no relationship with the establishment and the violence occurs during shoplifting, an attempted robbery, or a trespassing incident that turns violent.

Type Two: Customer/Client

Workplace violence that involves a customer or client usually occurs in organizations where there is high stress or emotions involved. The violence usually occurs in conjunction with the worker's normal duties, so this can be difficult to manage.

Type Three: Worker-to-Worker

Workplace violence can also occur between two or more employees within a company. More often than not, the reason for violence is personal, such as bullying, loss, trauma, or due to work-related conflicts. Common incidences of violence are made by former employees, but current employees can also cause issues.

Type Four: Domestic Violence

Workplace violence that involves an employee and their spouse or significant other can also be referred to as domestic violence that occurs in the workplace. This is when an employee's partner specifically targets them at work and this type of violence is often the most frequent as the abuser knows exactly where they will be and at what time.

Type Five: Ideological Violence

This type of workplace violence is usually carried out by an extremist person or people who want to make an ideological, religious, or political statement. Justifying their actions with their beliefs, their violent acts can range from mailed threats to bombs or Active Assailant situations.

It's important to understand that there are a number of motives and stressors that can cause a person to commit violence. As previously mentioned, some components to motive include, grievances at the workplace, at home, or other personal issues. Other motives can include ideological, political, or racially based, fame, and or mental health issues. It's important to note that mental health issues are not as prevalent as noted in the media. We will discuss warning signs of stressors in more detail in the following sections.

Situational Awareness

After every mass casualty situation, you hear two catch phrases: "we got have to be situationally aware," and "see something say something." These phrases are repeated over and over again; yet, their meaning is never explained. In this section, we will break down what these phrases actually mean.

Past. Present. Future.

Situational awareness is about you in relation to space and time. As the phrase *situational awareness* suggests, you need to be self-aware. This starts with understanding where you have been—your past. Why is this important? If you notice a situation in front of you and you know where you came from, then that is likely a safe place and direction to retreat to. Hopefully, as part of your past, you noticed good escape routes and safe places safe to go to.

You also need to be aware of where you currently are—your present. This means sights, sounds, routes, exits, safe places, potential hazards, individuals around you and their behavior, and anything *not normal*. Knowing your present will help you decide where to go and what decisions you may need to make, if a situation was to occur. This is also allows you to notice anything that is *not* normal and that my need to be reported, as the See Something, Say Something course of action recommends. I will discuss See Something, Say Something more in depth soon.

You should also be aware of the people around you. Often, we are too busy being plugged into our devices to lift our head and notice who is in front, behind, and to the left and right of us. The Boston Bombing was a prime example of people not paying attention to those around them. These two brothers were able to take their backpacks off, leave them in the middle of a crowd, and not one person noticed. Often, aside from going as far as leaving a backpack or package, assailants give off visual ques, which are noticeable if someone is looking and paying attention. This doesn't mean be paranoid of everyone around you, but pay attention; you may be standing next to the person about to commit mass murder.

Lastly, you need to know where you are going—your future. This is important for all the reasons previously mentioned. If you see a situation ahead of you, such as people running, smoke, sounds of gun fire or anything else *not normal*, retreat back to your past. Another possibility is if a situation is occurring in your past or present, you will need to exit ahead of you. Always pay attention to sights, sounds, routes, exits, safe places, potential hazards, individuals around you and their behavior, and anything *not normal.*

Let's talk briefly about your surrounds: Starting with Sights and Sounds, if you see people running, when it's not normal to be running, is that an indication that there is trouble? I would think so.

Sound: At every incident where there are gun shots or explosions, people usually say, "I thought it was fireworks" or "I thought a door was slammed," as in the case of the Manchester attack during an Ariana Grande concert. During this single attack, 22 innocent people were killed and up to 800 were injured. So, be aware of what is normal; ask yourself, is it normal for fireworks to be going off at work or inside a shopping mall?

It is pivotal to know where routes and exits are located because, if you have to evacuate, it helps to know where and how you will evacuate to. While in the mall, how often do you pay attention to where the closest exit is? Is it in your past, your present, or your future? Safe places can be somewhere that you can hide from an attacker, thus providing you some level of protection, be it cover or concealment—I will explain the differences later in the Action section. Potential hazards could affect your route selection and you don't want to end up causing more harm to yourself by running into a hazard that isn't the attacker, such as a construction zone.

Five Separate, yet Distinct Levels of Situational Awareness.

Tuned Out

When you are tuned out, you are completely unaware of your surroundings. Basically, you are on autopilot doing a normal routine. A prime example of this that we are all guilty of is driving home from work. How often do you really pay close attention to your drive home? Most of the time, it's been a long day and all you can think about is going home, right? This could also apply to those who are plugged into technology. A simple YouTube search can demonstrate this as people walk into fountains, street signs, or worse, all because they were not paying attention.

Relaxed Awareness

This is generally where I like to stay. You are paying attention, yet you are still enjoying life. You have a good understanding of your present, past, and future. Again, not paranoid but alert. Often, it is asked "how do I achieve this without being paranoid?" I admit, it is hard at first; however, once you train yourself, it becomes easy and second nature. I am frequently told that when I walk into a room, I own it. What do people mean by that? It's my awareness; when I arrive anywhere, I'm looking for my exits, I'm looking at who is around me, and I'm paying attention to behaviors. I'm not paranoid, I'm just situationally aware.

This didn't come naturally, and it is something I had to work on, but now I don't even notice I'm doing it. When I was in the military, we played a game that honestly anyone could play. We called it the K.I.M. game short for "Keep In Memory." We would be placed in a location for a random period of time, then had to leave that location. Once we left, we would have to describe as many things about that location and items in that location as possible in great detail.

Now, the question is: Can you do that in a non-military environment? Of course. Next time you walk into a room, restaurant, or store, look around and try to identify key points such as exit locations, how many people are there, what are they wearing, how many male and females, and any other items you think could be important. Once you leave, try to remember those details. If you are a manager or a teacher, you can do this during meetings with your staff or students.

When I was in an office, the manager and I held meetings; I would place ten non-descript random items on the desk in front of me. I would give my staff a break; then, once they came back in, I would ask them what was on the desk. Those who could name the most items and in the greatest detail got rewarded with gift cards. I would do this randomly and not at every meeting, yet at every meeting, my staff would be paying attention to everything. What they didn't realize was that this exercise had trained their mind to be situationally aware and not just during meetings.

Focused Awareness

Because you have been in a relaxed awareness state, you may notice something happening around you. You are now carefully observing what is going on around you. A good example of this is, for example, if you have ever been lost and ended up in the wrong neighborhood; in this case, chances are you had focused awareness.

High Alert

You have now gone from relaxed awareness, to focused awareness, and you have confirmed there is a threat and you need to take action. This is when the fight or flight instinct kicks in. The options of what actions you can take at this point depends on how much attention you had in the relaxed awareness and focused awareness.

Comatose

The human mind can be overloaded and, while you are conscious, your mind may become comatose and stops giving signals for your body to follow. This often happens when an individual is tuned out and an event happens; they skip all other levels and instantly become overwhelmed and fail to react.

There was a real scenario that I was involved with regarding an individual going into a comatose state. I was in Afghanistan working for Department of State Diplomatic Security Services, when we received a call that a local hotel was under attack. Upon arrival, aside from all the other chaos, me and a fellow team member noticed a woman in the lobby who was eating hummus. Despite all the explosions (car bomb and multiple suicide bombers), gunfire, and herself being wounded, her mind froze on the last conscious action, which was eating hummus. She was nonresponsive to us and we ultimately had to tackle her to provide her medical care. This goes to show that, even in a war zone where attacks happen daily, we can get complacent and think, it won't happen to me.

See Something, Say Something

Now that we are situationally aware, we can move on to the other catch phrase: see something, say something. Aside from the obvious, if you see an unaccompanied package or bag, what else should be seeing?

According to FBI studies of attackers, they find that there are three main areas that individuals generally display warning signs prior to an event taking place. Those warning signs include: speech, feelings, and behavior.

Speech
- Expression of suicidal tendencies

- Talking about previous violent incidents
- Unsolicited focus on dangerous weapons
- Paranoid thinking
- Overreaction to workplace changes

Feelings
- Depression or withdrawal
- Unstable, emotional responses
- Feeling either arrogant and supreme or powerless
- Intense anger or hostility

Behavior
- Use of, or increased use of alcohol or drugs
- Violations of company policies
- Increased absenteeism
- Exploiting or blaming others

In their speech, most attackers have been known to express suicidal tendencies or talk about previous violent incidents; they may begin to discuss dangerous weapons, become paranoid, and potentially overact to workplace changes. Noticing only one of these may not make the person a potential attacker; however, you should take notice and possibly report the behavior.

While an individual may express themselves using speech, they could manifest feelings, of depression or withdrawal; they may have unstable emotional responses, become arrogant, present themselves as being superior, or they may feel powerless. They may also show feelings of intense anger or hostility. Again, any one of these may not make them a future attacker, but you should take notice and report the behavior.

Lastly is behavior; some key behaviors to be aware of include increasing use of alcohol or drugs, violation of company policies, increased absenteeism, exploiting or blaming others. These are not normal behaviors, and if you notice them, they should be reported immediately.

Some additional warning signs include increasing erratic, unsafe, or aggressive behavior, hostile feelings of injustice or perceived wrongdoing, feeling marginalized from friends and colleagues, changes in work performance, sudden and dramatic changes in home life or personality, financial difficulties, pending civil or criminal litigation, observable grievances with threats or plans of retribution.

These are not independent of each other. Generally, individuals have feelings that will affect their behavior and speech. When you see a combination of these, you should report it immediately.

Pathway to Violence

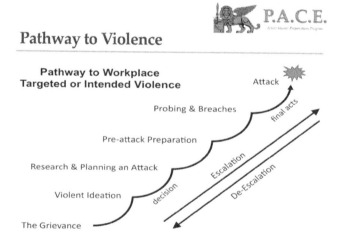

Systematic research and extensive case experience by Calhoun and Weston and others have demonstrated the central notion of a targeted pathway to violence and its significance for workplace violence risk assessment. Perpetrators of targeted violence consistently traverse the pathway to violence progressing along identifiable steps. Such movement is often revealed to others as it is not uncommon for the individual contemplating violence to communicate his or her feelings and intentions, in some form, to third parties such as co-workers, friends, and less often, directly to a target:

- It starts with a grievance of some kind, where thoughts begin, and ideas are formed in the individual's mind.

- It progresses to violent ideation or where they begin to form ideas and concepts. Thoughts are now replaced by action, declarative writing like a manifesto, and social media posts.

- Then, they begin to research and plan. Once they have researched a target, and planned how to strike that target, they move into pre-attack preparation where they devote time to gathering material and forewarning friends.

- Once they are ready, they begin to probe and breach by conducting surveillance and testing their plan. At this point, they can adjust their plan if needed; however, their intent is to strike. Last and final phase is the attack itself, when they implement their plan.

During any phase of the pathway to violence, it is possible to de-escalate and prevent a situation from occurring if the signs are recognized, and if individuals report what they have seen. This is critical if intervention is to take place to hopefully avoid a situation from occurring. You can look at any after-action review of most—if not all—Active Assailant, workplace violence or other mass casualty situations and you will see that warning signs were there, and yet, those that saw those signs said nothing. I don't know about you, but I wouldn't want that on my conscience. Now that we have an idea of what to look for and we understand the pathway to violence, we can move on to an example.

Let's say that I am a salesman at an organization, and for the past two years I have been the top salesman of that organization. I have always maintained high standards when it comes to performance, attendance, appearance, and attitude. Let's say you are my supervisor or a co-worker and you notice that I am starting to come in late, I have missed a few days of work, I appear to not have shaved, my poor hygiene is becoming noticeable, and my clothes are looking a bit disheveled. One or more of these can be an indicator that something is wrong in my life, personally or professionally. Clearly, this is not my normal behavior and the change is noticeable. There are two options on how this situation can be approached:

- My supervisor can address me in a stern fashion writing me up and giving me notice that this not tolerated and not acceptable.
- I could be approached by my supervisor or colleagues in a way that would help and show me that they care.

The first scenario could be enough to push a me over the edge and be that proverbial straw that breaks the camel's back. The second option might just stop me from turning into a mass murderer—this is an extreme example, but I think you can see my point.

You may not know why or what is causing someone to change their behavior, but we need to recognize that there has been a change and take positive action. The point is that we need to acknowledge these red flags or warning signs and do something. Too often, only *after* a situation has occurred do people reflect back and say "oh yeah he/she did seem a bit off and not their normal self." It is easy to ignore problems when they aren't yours, but someone else's problems could become your problem in the worst way possible.

Now that we have discussed an individual's speech, feelings, and behavior there are a few more items that we need to address regarding See Something Say Something. In the case of Columbine and in a very small part of the San Bernardino shooting, bullying was noted as being a catalyst for the events that took place. Most adults think of bullying to be a school-age issue, but it can also be done by adults. Over time, bullying can push people into a mindset that they normally would never go to. It is important that, if any form of bullying is suspected or witnessed, it is reported immediately.

Suspicious packages or unoccupied bags should also be reported immediately. During the Boston marathon, two backpacks were left in a crowd of people and resulted in six deaths and 264 injured. What if someone would have reported them? Could they have been in time to save some of those who were killed or possibly reduced the number of injured?

Lastly are social media posts. Those that look to harm others, often post their intentions. In those same FBI reports they find indicators of the pathway to violence can be seen on individual social media accounts—some is very obvious and some not so much, but it's still there.

The key to remember is:

Reporting

I have discussed what you should report, but now the question is *how* and *where*? There are multiple ways to report something outside of the workplace. Most states, counties, cities, towns, and local police departments have a toll-free number you can contact. Each location is different, so you would need to look up what the local resource for your area is. If you can't find a local resource Department of Homeland Security and the FBI both have toll-free numbers that you can call.

Within organizations, there should be a reporting procedure as well. That procedure could be anonymous and could come in many forms. A toll-free number could be established and there are many ways to have that monitored 24 hours a day, 7 days a week. A reporting email account could easily be set up to receive and log reports of suspicious activity. An organization may also have an open-door policy, where any employee is free to go to management and report what they have seen. Whatever the procedure is, it should be simple, people should know about it, and everyone should be encouraged to use it.

If you don't already know, they you should take the time to find out what your organizations procedure is. If they don't have one, this is a good opportunity for you to recommend that they create one for your safety and the safety of others.

Security Procedures

Let's discuss what companies and leaders can do to help prepare for, and potentially reduce, the chances of an Active Assailant situation. The better prepared you are, the higher the survivability possibility, and the harder target you present, thus reducing the chances of said event.

Risk assessment consists of an objective evaluation of risk—the magnitude of the potential loss (L), and the probability (p) that the loss will occur—in which assumptions and uncertainties are clearly considered and presented.

Vulnerability assessments is a process that defines, identifies, and classifies security gaps.

A **policy** is a guiding principle used to set direction in an organization.

A **procedure** is a series of steps to be followed to meet the stated policy.

A **crisis management plan** elaborates the actions to be taken by management, as well as employees, during emergency situations.

A **risk management plan** is used to foresee risks, estimate impacts, and define responses to issues. This is generated once a proper risk assessment has been completed.

Facility security measures are a combination of physical barriers and site hardening; physical entry and access controls; security lighting; intrusion detection systems; video surveillance; security personnel; and security policies and procedures.

An **incident response team** is a group of people who prepare for and respond to any emergency incident, and are ideally trained and prepared to fulfill the roles required by the situation—for example, to serve as incident commander, medical assistant, or media liaison. This is not a team that should be thrown together to theoretically solve a problem. Before an organization choose this as an option, there are multiple considerations that need to be addressed:

- This is a special niche within security services, which requires special skills sets
- Requires larger team to set up and operate
- Recruitment considerations of the team members:
  - Background
  - Physical fitness
  - Overall ability and capability
- Team management requires specific management skills
- Specific and ongoing training is required
- Specific SOPs (Standard Operating Procedures) need to be developed, tested, reevaluated, and revised
- Local law enforcement inclusion is a must
- Potential liabilities need to be addressed with legal and insurance

Mutual support agreements are made between organizations promising that, if an event were to occur, the other would assist in manufacturing product, or servicing clients until the affected organization had recovered enough to resume their operations. This helps business resilience in maintaining business operations.

Facility considerations can be addressed using the acronym **CPTEB** (Crime Prevention Through Environmental Design). This is simply using landscaping, access control, crowd/group management, and area maintenance to your advantage created, defined, and defensible space.

Employee background checks are critical and should be conducted during the hiring processes and, depending on the position, a recurring event to monitor the quality of employees. Internal and interagency information sharing is just as important in the civilian sector as it is in the government sector. It's critical that Human Resources share information to the Security Department in regards to employees and the potential for a situation to occur. It's just as critical for Security Departments to share information with local law enforcement if/when needed.

It's important that local law enforcement be invited to visit your organization. This has many benefits: first, it builds a strong relationship between the business and local law enforcement; second, it allows those police officers to get to know the layout of your facility, which could come in handy if an event were to occur; third, this makes your locations a harder target—if someone was thinking about using your location for an event and they see that police agencies are often visiting, their success would be greatly diminished and they are likely to select another target.

We have already discussed the social media aspect; however, it is important to note that organizations can also monitor social media sites and threads, and report to the authorities any suspicious activity without violating a person's rights and freedoms.

Access Control Measures

What is access control measure that we can prepare ahead of time? Access control will vary depending on the type of business, location, and other factors that affect how your organization interacts with customers and vendors. Let's start by understanding what a barrier is: A barrier is an obstacle intended to block movement or access. Security guards, administrative assistants, and other organization staff members are barriers. Doors and windows can be obstacles, but without a locking device, they merely slow a person down and don't stop entry.

Door locks come in many forms and fashions, to include locks that require keys and electronic door locks that require an access card. To keep up with current times, electronic door locks are the preferred method to lock doors. A benefit to having an electronic door lock is that the access point can remain locked at all times. This is possible since an individual who has clearance to enter would have an access card or code to enter as needed. With that said, a critical error that companies make is to not delete access after an employee has been terminated or resigned.

Another benefit is if the organization requires the doors to remain unlocked, because if there is an event, those doors can be locked remotely using software that accompanies that locking device. This is especially useful in a school environment, because if there is an Active Assailant, administrators can lock down the entire campus all at once.

There is one issue I'd like to address regarding electronic locks. If the doors are locked either by an individual or a system-wide lockdown, and if a fire alarm is tripped, all locks automatically become unlocked. This is mandated by national fire safety codes, so do keep that in mind and be prepared to utilize other materials to block the door, if needed.

Having visible IDs also helps with access control. A good company policy is that all employees and visitors must have an ID visible at all times. This goes back to See Something, Say Something. If you see someone without an ID, it is an indicator that the person might not belong there and needs to be reported immediately.

Entry oversite can be done utilizing cameras where someone sees the individual requesting access prior to letting that them in. It can also be done by having security personnel or staff check individuals in prior to granting access. Best case is that you have both video checks prior to gaining entry, then once the individual has entered, security personnel or staff check that individual in. This method is best used in conjunction with company policy that all visitor names are to be submitted to the point of entry prior to their arrival and, if the names are not submitted, the person is either denied access or has to wait for higher approval.

Access control should have multiple layers of policy and procedure, such as:

- Key log who has received keys
- Why type of keys they received
- What type of access they were granted
- Outside visitor access procedures
- Zero tolerance to tailgating, one person or one car in at a time, no exceptions
- Resignation or termination key or access card collection or deletion
- Emergency lock down procedures

Being prepared to access management is critical in reducing the potential for an Active Assailant situation. If they can't get in, they can't cause injury. As an individual, there are some additional access control measures you can do as well. By arranging your desk or desks to not be directly in front of the door, you give yourself a better chance to react. Also, by not having your back facing the entry way, you can be more situationally aware of who enters your work space.

You could create a mini hallway by the door or point of entry. Many times, offices or classrooms have filing cabinets, which could be placed in a position to slow down an attacker. Can you, or have you, identified potential barricades that you could use to block doorways and entrances if there was an Active Assailant event? Identifying these objects ahead of time is great, but do not forget to test your theory of how you would use them. Sometimes, what you will find is that what seems like a good idea, doesn't work at all, so train on it to ensure success if the time comes.

If you work in a school, what are your lockdown procedures? Do you even have procedures? A few recommendations to have in your lockdown procedures would include how will you communicate the lockdown to staff and local law enforcement? Do you have a third party alert software that can do this for you once initiated? Do you have a signal or code words that staff can use to indicate distress? How will doors and access points lock? If you have electric locks, can they be integrated in with a third party alert software? Have you established safe areas, where they are, and how many people can they hold? How will you account for staff or students? Once lockdown is initiated, is everyone aware that doors are to remain locked and shut until the police arrive?

These are just a few issues that should be addressed if you have a lockdown policy.

Training

A key area that needs to be focused on during the Prepare phase is training. You can have all the policies and procedures, risk management tools and crisis management plans, but if you don't train on them, then they are as worthless as the paper they are printed on.

Preparedness training, such as the P.A.C.E. program, helps organizations focus in on areas that they might not have thought about. As the saying goes, you don't know what you don't know. These programs can help identify gaps in plans and provide suggestions on how to better current plans.

Table top training is a great way to get leaders focused on identifying any gaps in procedures and talk through what actions should be taken during an event. This is also a great way to incorporate first responders, so they have a clear understanding of the organizations plan.

Drills and rehearsals are also essential; however, it's important to know the difference. Training drills are conducted with a limited number of people knowing when and how it is to occur. Rehearsals are pre-planned and everyone involved is well aware ahead of time that this training is to take place. I like to think of this as the Crawl-Walk-Run. The crawl phase is the table top exercise; the walk phase is when you do full rehearsals; the run phase is when you conduct the drill to confirm the information has been disseminated and retained at the lowest level.

As we have discussed earlier, having advanced medical training can only benefit the organization. Medical training provided by certified instructors can help reduce liability and save lives if an incident were to occur. To be clear, there is a difference between First Aid and Trauma Care; the advance courses to be considered are BCON (Bleeding Control), TECC (Tactical Emergency Casualty Care), and TCCC (Tactical Combat Causality Care).

Once training has been conducted, it must be documented. If it's not documented, it hasn't occurred. This is important for liability issues and also to ensure that all employees have met the training requirements and that the training they have is current and up to date. Items that should be documented are: Time, date of the training, location of the training, basic employee information of who attended the training, the type of training received, and who provided the training—you might want to add contact details for the training provider as well.

All this training helps to create what is called Force Multipliers. Simply put, you are able to generate more output with limited resources. For example, if you have one person who has taken advance medical training, if an incident occurs, that person can now direct a number of others without medical training to help and assist with the wounded, thus increasing the output of medical support without having additional medically trained individuals.

As a quick note on who you select as a trainer, make sure that they are qualified to teach the subject they are instructing you on. You wouldn't expect to receive a class on computer security from the building maintenance supervisor, would you? You should also not expect someone with little to no background in Active Assailant training to provide you a class on that very subject. Last note on training: Training reinforces behavior and also advocates a strong Active Assailant/Workplace Violence program, which can be a deterrence.

How can the Civilian population better prepare themselves for an Active Assailant incident? One way is by taking preparedness training such as P.A.C.E. (Prepare, Action, Care, and Evacuate) provided by Security Concepts Group LLC. As you will see, these courses give you information on how to prepare for and react to an Active Assailant situation.

Crisis management training is often overlooked. ASIS provides webinars and in-person seminars, along with books and recommendations, for standards that are invaluable. Organizations and leadership can develop their own site-specific crisis management plans; without a plan, how will anyone know what actions need to be taken if an event was to occur?

Table top training is a great and cost-effective way to validate your plans and find areas that need improvement. Don't forget to invite government agencies as well; this will allow them to know your plan and how they can fit in to assist. Cautionary note: When including local law enforcement, have realistic expectations. They will come speak to your organization about statistics, Run-Hide-Fight, and possibly do an exercise utilizing your employees as role players. The main point of that training is for the law enforcement to practice how they will make entry and "shoot, move, and communicate." They also do not discuss topics covered so far in this book, in regards to prevention. They teach from the aspect of being in the moment, which in my professional opinion is very one dimensional.

If you do outsource instructors, do your due diligence. Make sure they are qualified to be the subject matter experts on this topic, or any other topics they may be teaching. Important topics should be left for professionals and not just to someone who has attended a seminar or two.

Critical Items

Some critical items that must be prepared ahead of time include the prepositioning of trauma medical equipment—a trauma bag is an essential piece of equipment when it comes to saving lives during an Active Assailant event. This is not a First Aid kit and its contents will be discussed during the

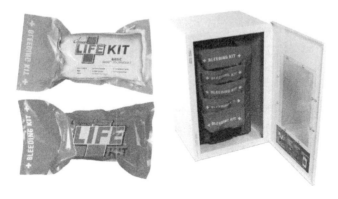

Care portion of this training. As leadership within an organization, if you have this medical equipment it will serve no purpose if individuals at the lowest level do not know about it or do not know of its location. As a staff member in an organization, it is important that you ask your supervisor and managers where these bags are located. The best recommendation is that trauma bags be prepositioned and co-located with all AEDs (Automatic External Defibrillator) you may have on site.

Every Organization should have detailed floor plans and escape routes, not only because it is a OSHA requirement, but also because it is important to include well defined assembly areas, plans for Emergency Operation Centers (EOC), and identify potential triage areas. Each of these locations must have their own size, space, and capability requirements. For example, EOC needs power supply or room for temporary power supplies and space for multiple agencies such as local law enforcement, Department of Home Land Security, FEME, FBI, and other agencies that may respond depending on the severity of the situation.

Crisis management plans need to be accessible as they will provide critical direction on what needs to be done during and immediately after an event has occurred.

Within the crisis management plan there should be a communication plan, which outlines the specific incident management chain of command. It should also prove predetermined code words or signals used to indicate an incident is occurring. It can also provide the procedures of activating any third party alert software and hardware that might be installed at your facility.

Alert software is a great tool that has been introduced into the market. It allows administrators to send out mass alerts via text, email, desktop phones, and instant messages on computers. It simultaneously alerts the authorities, and simplifies the notification process. After all, the quicker the first responders arrive, the sooner the event will end and potentially more lives can be saved.

Some additional items that you could prepare ahead of time are supplemental door locking devices. There are plenty on the market to choose from and finding which one is right will depend on the door, type of handle, and how the door opens. There are also ballistic countermeasures that can be considered. Kevlar can be added to walls, and doors to elevate protection. This can be done without being noticeable, thus keeping the work space looking like an office and not like a military secure compound. Windows can also be either replaced with complete bullet resistant glass or ballistic laminate can be added to existing glass. Laminate will not provide nearly the same level of protection, but it will provide just enough that individuals may have the chance to react and take appropriate action.

Mindset: **Recognize that there is the potential of workplace violence, Active Assailants, or other emergency situations.**

Act

*Life is 10% what happens to you
and 90% how you react to it.*
— Charles R Swindoll

Through all my experiences, this quote has been a guiding principle that has gotten me through some tough situations. In this section, we will discuss the Run-Hide-Fight as well as other topics. Keep in mind there is no set rule on when you are to do each action or that you need to do those actions in any particular order. We will also discuss motivation, OODA Loop, and using firearms as a defense.

Motivation

During a workplace violence or Active Assailant situation, you have to decide that you want to live. Of course, we all want to live, but facing life-threating situations people can panic, and freeze so, how can we get in the right mindset ahead of time? That process starts by thinking about what motivates you to survive.

Often, after an incident, survivors state that all they thought about was their parents, their children, their family, their faith. Bottom line is you have to have the right mindset and decide you want to live and survive by any means necessary. Use those that are important to you as motivator to make it through the situation, even when you don't think you can draw power from them to get you through the situation. You must decide you want to live.

OODA Loop

This is part of our natural decision-making process, but it's vital to understand it as it relates to Active Assailant situations. What does OODA Loop stands for?

O: **Observe**; this is your basic situational awareness, using your major senses, such as sight, sound, or smell, you become aware that something is not right. For example:

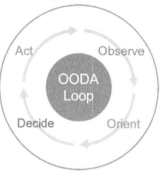

- You could see someone running with a weapon or see a crowd running
- You could hear gun shots, yelling, screaming, someone shouting commands
- You could smell smoke or gunpowder

- Any one of these should be an indicator that something is not right

O: Orientate; this is situational understanding, where are you in relation to the threat or disturbance? Where are you in relation to a door lock, exit, hiding space, potential weapon, barricade materials?

D: Decide; once you observed there is a threat, and you have orientated yourself, you then have to decide what your best option for survival is.

A: Act; you now need to take action based on the best option you have decided will give you maximum chance of survival. As we stated previously, once you commit to an act, commit 100%.

One thing to also think about is your decision-making process can often have an effect on the attacker's decision-making process. For example, you observe there is an attacker, you orientate yourself to the door, decide to lock the door, and act on locking the door. If the attacker observed your door, orientated towards your door, decided to enter that door, and went into your space, if the door is locked, the attacker who had decided to act, now has to start their decision-making process all over again, thus giving you time, and time for first responders to arrive. Keep in mind that an attacker's time is limited and they generally follow the path of least resistance, unless they are targeting a specific person. If you have disrupted their OODA Loop, you have bought yourself more time, and you have given first responders more time to find, engage, and neutralize the threat. That's a simple example but you can see how it could be beneficial to you.

Run

Everyone says I'm just going to take off and run out of there as soon as an event starts, but it's important to talk about a few issues.

First, you should have a plan and take a second to come up with an escape route. This is important because you don't want to be caught out in the open or at a dead end, which causes you to back to where you just came from. If you are in a hallway, you want to follow the walls to void congestion. If you are in the hallway when it begins, get out of the hallway immediately either by exiting the building or by entering a room. It's important that you leave your belongings behind—is your purse or laptop worth your life? You should bring co-workers and customers with you, but if they refuse, then you will need to leave them. Again, once you have decided to act and run, you need to commit 100%.

Second, be creative to get out. Windows offer a great escape route, even if they need to be broken. If you are on the

second or even third floor, there are affordable, easy-to-use ladders that can connect to any window for a safe decent to the ground floor. The key is to be creative and find a way out, no matter what it is. As you are running, keep your hands visible, you never know if you will run into a first responder and you want to indicate that you are not a threat. On a positive note, handguns may be easily concealed but they can be hard to aim, especially under stress.

Hide

If you decide to hide, there are a few things you should know and do. First, you need to know the difference between cover and concealment: Cover will limit the attacker's ability to see you and provide limited protection against gun fire; Concealment will only block the attacker's ability to see you. (this picture, produced by Department of Homeland Security, is a poor example of how to hide).

For example, hiding behind a concreate wall or a heavy piece of machinery will block the attacker's ability to see you and can also provide you protection if they shoot in your direction. If you hide under a desk, this will merely block the ability to see you, and if they shoot into the desk, the bullets will go through the desk and likely strike you. You want to put as much distance and objects as possible between you and the attacker. If you hide in a closet, do not stand directly behind the door, as it is only concealment and if bullets are fired into the door, you will be hit. Instead, once you are in the closet, take a step left of right away from the door with the intention of hopefully having a wall to your back that is towards the attacker. If you enter a room, office, or closet, *lock* the doors if possible and barricade yourself inside. Again, you want to put as much stuff in between you and the attacker as possible.

This picture depicts a training scenario. A few observations can be made.

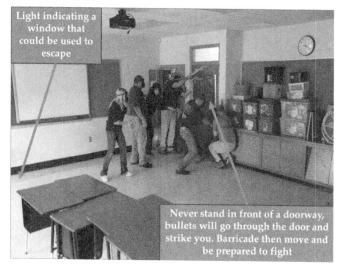

Light indicating a window that could be used to escape

Never stand in front of a doorway, bullets will go through the door and strike you. Barricade then move and be prepared to fight

- Lighting indicates that there is a window. What we do not know is if this classroom is on the ground level or multiple floors up. If it is on the ground level, then exiting through a broken window would be a viable option.
- Everyone is huddled up behind the door; if the assailant were to shoot into the door all of them would be struck, wounded, and possibly die.
- No one is preparing to fight, there are plenty of items in the room that could make acceptable weapons.

This picture highlights the need to think outside of the box and come up with solutions that are not normally thought of. Remember you have the rest of your life to make decisions and choices that could decide if you live or die. Once you are in the room, do not allow anyone to leave or enter until the location has been cleared by law enforcement. Even if things go quiet, stay in the safe location; the police will find you and get you. The last thing you want to do is exit assuming the site is clear when it really is not. Silence your cell phones—we will go into more detail later on what information to provide to 911; however, if you are hiding, you do not want the ringing of your phone to give away you position. Stay as low as possible; this reduces your target size, increasing your survivability if being shot at. Keep in mind you must be prepared to fight. If the attacker enters the space that you are hiding in, you very well may have to fight so prepare for that.

Other example: Imagine there is an Active Assailant situation, you are safe and secure in your classroom, and the shooting stops. Your instinct is to exit with your students, which is a fair and normal response. However, have you thought about what the children are potentially about to see when they exit? While you are safe, start to think of the exit strategy, meaning how are you going to protect the kids psychologically from seeing their friends dead in the hallway covered in blood? Although the students know an event has occurred, they haven't truly seen the aftermath, which will have a much more long-lasting effect than if they didn't see anything at all. So, think about how you will protect them from seeing things they will never forget. A preventative measure would be waiting for law enforcement to clear the location, until they come get you. When they arrive, ask them what the scene is like and what route you should take to avoid the visual aftermath.

You may not be able to avoid walking past the carnage, but you can at least give directions, such as instructing students to look at the wall when you exit or have them hold hands and close their eyes as you exit.

Fight

Fighting should only take place when it's your last re-sort and overwhelmingly possible that you are going to die if you do nothing. You must consider the probability of *your* death, available re-sources, and the total risk.

If fighting is your only op-tion and the assailant is the immediate area, your best chance of survival is to swarm attack. Get as many people to join you and attack as possible. The risk of injury is great, but the potential of death by doing nothing might be greater. If you decide or are forced to fight, then as mentioned before, commit 100%. Think outside of the box on what can be used as a weapon. Depending on your environment, weapons can vary. If you have the right mindset that *anything* can be a weapon, you have a higher probability of success. Anything can be used to hit or thrown and many items can be used as a stabbing device. Some weapons could include keys used as stabbing devices, laptops can be used to club the attacker, and chairs can be thrown.

Remember that even if you don't harm the attacker right away, you are creating time when they are not accurately shooting because they are being forced to protect themselves. That's when you close the distance and really inflict damage, disarm, and stop the killing.

One example I like to use is the fire extinguisher. I have always seen government videos or heard people say to use the fire extinguisher as a weapon to hit the attacker. This is a great choice of a weapon, but the execution is slightly flawed. If you try to hit the attacker with a fire extinguisher, chances are you may get shot. However, if you first discharge that fire extinguisher in the attacker's direction, the attacker will begin to choke, and his vision will be greatly impaired, thus providing you a greater possibility of success, meaning you live another day.

In the fight scenario, you have the rest of your life to win—if you think about this ahead of time. before a situation occurs, you will be better prepared and have a better chance as surviving.

Last thing on fighting is to keep in mind that, regardless of whether you have chosen to run or hide, you may still need to fight. So, as you choose your course of action, you must always be ready to go on the attack to survive. Just because you hide, doesn't mean the attacker won't enter your space. You basically have a few options: Hope they don't find you and shoot you; fight and attack. Remember you have to decide you want to live by any means necessary. By attacking the attacker, you severely disrupt their OODA Loop and decision-making process and now you are in control.

Use of Fire Arms

Let's address the use of fire arms to neutralize an Active Assailant from the perspective of a regular civilian with a

Concealed Carry Permit.[3] To be prepared as a civilian, you must have years of training. Even then, depending on the type of training, it may not be enough to save your life or the lives of others. Training has to be realistic, situational, and not just shooting coke cans out in the desert. Keeping in mind that, if you have to take that shot, your heart rate will be elevated, you may be breathing hard, your stress level will be at levels you may have never encountered, and many other physiological conditions will affect your accuracy. You must be hyper situationally aware; you need to know how many assailants there are, where they are, what types of fire arms they have, and if they have any body armor. If you can't answer these questions, then you might want to leave it to the professionals.

If you have the training as a civilian, you still need to consider if you are physiologically prepared to engage a human target: What if you miss? What if you shoot an innocent person? What will you do once first responders arrive? Put yourself in their shoes; there is an Active Assailant event and you are armed. That's all they know. What do you think a potential outcome is? Even if they don't shoot you, which they very well might, they need to secure you, thus taking time away from going after and neutralizing the real threat. Unless the threat is immediately in front of you, leave it to the professionals, and never chase down the threat. You don't know if they have explosive devices or if there are multiple assailants. You could be running into a worse scenario than you originally thought.

---

3 Disclaimer: I am a huge supporter of the second amendment and I believe in the right to bear arms, but some serious thought and consideration needs to be addressed. This professional opinion is a broadbrush opinion and by no means do I believe that regular folks can't and haven't successfully stopped Active Assailants.

A big topic for debate is whether teachers should be armed or not. Let me counter that question with my own: Do you think an armed teacher is physiologically prepared to stop a student who has become an Active Assailant? Do you think that teacher would try to first reason with the student who they may know and have a relationship with, or will they take the necessary steps to stop the assailant? What if they try to reason and negotiate with the assailant, which is more than the action they will take? This will more than likely result in the teacher being shot, thus giving an additional weapon to the assailant and leaving students unprotected and without guidance. There are several other arguments that can be made for and against, but this is one point of view I rarely hear being discussed.

As a tragic example of a private citizen with a Conceal Carry Permit, Joseph Wilcox was killed on June 8, 2014. An active shooter entered a Walmart, fired a shot at the ceiling and ordered shoppers to leave. Joseph Wilcox, who was carrying a concealed weapon, drew his weapon and followed the attacker, failing to see the attacker's wife, not realizing she was armed and an accomplice. As Mr. Wilcox followed the husband, the wife followed him, and when Mr. Wilcox was about to shoot, she fired first. He never saw it coming and died instantly. What Mr. Wilcox didn't know is that this couple had no intentions of killing innocent civilians,

which is why the husband initially fired his gun in the air instead of at Walmart customers. He was also unaware this couple just shot and killed two Las Vegas Metro police officers and their intention was to kill as many Metro officers as possible. Joseph Wilcox had the best intentions, but paid the ultimate price. I don't mention this story to point out what he did wrong, but I use it as a situation we could all learn from. When I sat in a briefing by members of Las Vegas Metro PD on this event and saw the video of his murder, I thought to myself that it could have been me, because I might have taken the same actions.

What actions you take during an Active Assailant event—right, wrong or indifferent—is ultimately your decision. Some of you who read this book have the experience, skills, and ability to neutralize a threat using a weapon, but these are exceptions and not the rule. As I like to say, when you decide to act, commit to it 100%.

Care

Act as if what you do makes a difference. It does. – William James

Did you know that many casualties in an Active Assailant event die from treatable wounds? Unfortunately, there is no current statistic on how many casualties actually die due to treatable wounds, but consider that, in every Active Assailant situation, there are only three categories:

- Alive
- Dead
- Wounded

I can assure you that no assailant is so accurate that each person they shoot, stab, blow up or run over, dies instantly. If you or other individuals had the proper tools and training to take care of those who are injured, how many lives could be saved?

This section is to empower the immediate responder—you—to take action as soon as possible. We will discuss techniques that meet the standards of the National Association of Emergency Medical Technicians (NAEMT). However, you will *not* be certified as a medical practitioner at the end of this section. There are plenty of courses that individuals can take, starting with the most basic course of Bleeding Control. This is generally a free course and most the material covered in this section is taught with the addition of hands-on training.[4]

Before you can consider treating any wounded, you need to first make sure the situation itself is safe to do so. Many times, individuals are

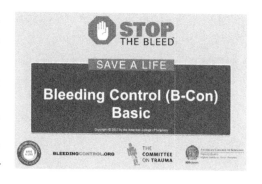

quick to help others without the current situation being secure and they end up becoming casualties themselves. In other words, don't be a hero!

---

4 Information on where you can find a hands-on Bleeding Control training course near you can be found at www.bleedingcontrol.org

Primary Principles of Immediate Response

According to Bleeding Control course, American College of Surgeons, and NAEMT, these are the basic principles that should govern your response if you find yourself in one of these situations:

- First, make sure the scene is safe. You must ensure your own safety before trying to help someone else.
- ABCs of Bleeding:
  - ALERT. Get help. Call or have someone call 911 for assistance. Make every effort to assure help is on the way as you proceed to the next step.
  - BLEEDING. Look for the site of the bleeding, as it will frequently dictate how you will need to control it.
  - COMPRESSION. Once you have located the source, control of the bleeding will involve the application of direct pressure, the placement of a tourniquet, the packing of an open wound, or a combination of all of these techniques.

Safety

Your personal safety is an important consideration. If you become injured as well, you won't be able to help anyone and the situation you find yourself in becomes more complicated. If the scene in not safe for whatever reason, you should remove yourself (and the victim, if possible) from danger and try to find a safe location. Once you reach safety, you can focus on bleeding control.

Exposure to an injured patient's blood or other body fluids is another safety consideration. Blood-borne pathogens are germs that could be spread through exposure to someone else's blood. If you have access to bleeding control supplies, you should also have access to protective gloves. If these supplies are not available to you, wash your hands thoroughly after touching a victim and ask EMS personnel about appropriate blood cleanup procedures.

Alert

Calling your local emergency services is one of the most important actions you can take when someone is injured. This will start the process of getting trained responders to the location off the incident. It is critical, therefore, that you make every effort to call 911 or direct someone at the scene to do so as soon as possible. This is also extremely important when the situation involves any criminal activity, as it will also initiate a police response to the scene.

Bleeding

The sooner the bleeding site is controlled, the better the chances of survival. The first step is to identify the source of the bleeding. This requires a careful inspection to identify the site of bleeding. In some cases, the source of blood loss is obvious. In other cases, you may need to open or remove clothing to find the injury. The following steps should be followed:

Find where the victim is bleeding from
- Open or remove the clothing so you can see the woun
- Look for and identify life-threatening bleeding
- Blood that is spurting out of the wound
- Blood that won't stop coming out of the wound
- Blood that is pooling on the ground
- Clothing that is soaked with blood
- Bandages that are soaked with blood
- Loss of all or part of an arm or leg
- Bleeding in a victim who is now confused or unconscious

Compression: Stop the Bleeding

Direct pressure can control bleeding from anywhere on the body. A firmly applied pair of hands placed directly onto a bleeding wound can control arterial bleeding, even from large blood vessels, such as those in the neck and groin. Remember you must hold pressure until you are relieved by the medical responders arriving to the scene. You should not release the pressure to see how well it is working. Just keep pushing firmly on the wound to control the bleeding. Applying pressure to a bleeding wound is a painful procedure and will hurt the victim but it is necessary in order to stop the bleeding.

The Basics

According to the National Association of Emergency Medical Technicians the average loss of life due to blood loss occurs within two–four minutes. This is important to understand since it highlights how critical every second is. Generally, you should automatically deduct at least one minute from that time since you are not likely to be providing care immediately after the wound is inflicted. Keep in mind that the current statistics vary on police response time; however, they generally arrive within four–seven minutes after the 911 call is received. Upon arriving, the first priority for law enforcement is to neutralize the threat, not tend to the wounded or evacuate individuals, which makes it clear why this section of information is critical for the survival of any victims who are severely wounded. If no care is rendered by those in the immediate area, the potential for loss of life is almost guaranteed.

Here is a prime example of the importance of individuals being able to provide immediate care for those that are wounded: On June 12, at 2:02 a.m., the Orlando Police received the first notification of shots fired at Pulse Night club in Orlando Florida. At 2:12 a.m. a Ms. Akyra Murray called her mother begging for help and stated that she and her cousin had been shot while hiding in a bathroom stall with others. Ms. Murry later died from her wounds and became the youngest victim to die in the Pulse Night club shooting. This situation ended at 5:53 a.m., almost four hours after the initial shooting and killing began.

This is one example of where a victim succumbed to their wounds because no treatment was given, or inadequate treatment was given. Is it possible that if some basic life saving techniques were applied, she and others may still be alive? As you will see, the Care topic is critical to survival. Most other active shooter or Active Assailant training tell you to provide aid, but they don't tell you how and why. We have discussed the why and now we will discuss the how. Topics we will cover include:

- Types of aid
- Hemorrhage locations
- Direct pressure
- Medical supply familiarization
- Alternative medical supplies
- Wound packing
- Pressure dressing
- CPR considerations

I'll start with a basic question: Who cares for the wounded and potentially saves lives until Emergency Medical Services Arrives? The answer is *you*.

Types of Aid

First there are three types of aid that can be rendered:

- **Self-Aid.** This is the process of treating your own wounds. This is an important step in saving your own life. Life threatening wounds can be treated if quick action is taken. I have personally seen individuals place  tourniquets on themselves to stop their own bleeding, which in turn saved their lives.

- **Buddy Aid.** This is the act of assisting the injured in order to treat their wounds and potentially save their life.

- **Medic-Aid.** This is the professional medical treatment administered by a trained medical professional.

Causes of Preventable Death Today

Let's discuss the main causes of preventable death today. Depending on your age, you might remember being taught the ABCs, or Airway Breathing and Circulation. This has been proven to be an obsolete order of treatment.

- Research has shown that hemorrhage from extremity wounds is the number one cause of preventable death. If you remember it only takes two–four minutes before a person bleeds to death. Tourniquets are the easiest and most effective ways to stop someone from bleeding to death when it comes to severe extremity wounds.
- Junctional hemorrhage is bleeding from the groin, shoulder, and neck. You can only apply pressure to stop the bleeding and you cannot apply a tourniquet.

- Non-compressible hemorrhage wounds are wounds to the abdomen; you cannot apply pressure and you cannot apply a tourniquet.
- Tension pneumothorax or sucking chest wound is when air is caught in the chest cavity, which collapse the lung, thus preventing the ability to breathe.
- Airway problems, the inability to breathe due to head and neck wounds or chocking.

Our main focus will be on tourniquets and pressure dressings for extremity wounds and wound packing. During an Active Assailant event, there is only one medical treatment you should be worried about: Stopping massive hemorrhages, meaning heavy arterial bleeding or bright red or spurting blood.

Hemorrhage Control

Extremity Wounds

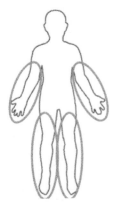

Wounds involving life-threatening bleeding from an extremity are managed by application of a tourniquet, and in conjunction with pressure dressings. These can be applied either by the victim themselves or by a partner. This procedure needs to be accomplished as soon as possible.

Junctional Areas

Junctional areas are those where a tourniquet cannot be applied to—neck, armpit, or groin. Wounds to these areas can
be controlled by packing the wound
with gauze, Kerlex or alternatively cotton clothing material; then, apply direct
pressure over the wound. This type of
hemorrhage control takes time, usually from three to ten minutes of direct
pressure.

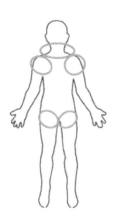

Central Chest, Abdomen

Wounds to the central part of the body—
chest and abdomen—cause internal
injuries that cannot be addressed on
location. In order to stop bleeding, the
patient must be transported to the closest appropriate trauma center for evaluation and likely operation. Therefore, it
is important to recognize these wounds
and notify EMS when they arrive.

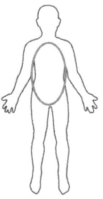

Unlike extremity and junctional
wounds, you cannot pack or apply pressure to injuries that
are larger than gunshot or shrapnel wound—basically the size
of a quarter. For large abdominal wounds, all you can do is
cover and apply a light pressure bandage. Rapid transport is
critical. Wounds that are internal can be tender to the touch
and there may be discoloration of the affected area. One example of potential internal injuries would be injuries caused
from a blast or explosion. You might not see the wound but

the pressure from the blast could rupture organs, meaning it can be just as deadly as a severe extremity or junctional bleed.

Direct Pressure

This will apply to all wounds, except central cavity wounds that are larger than a gun shot or shrapnel. Direct pressure should be an *immediate* response to heavy  hemorrhage. Even if the patient requires a tourniquet, the immediate first response should be to slow the rate of blood loss that is occurring. Every second counts, so applying direct pressure while getting a tourniquet prepared could be the difference between life and death. You can do that by applying large amounts of pressure to the areas above the wound site. This needs to be done as you are preparing a tourniquet.

Direct pressure can be applied by finger, hands, or knee, and it works most of the time on external bleeding, but it does take time. At a minimum you need, three–four minutes, although ten minutes is preferred. If it's possible, elevate the wound; this decreases the amount of blood flow to the affected area, this also slows the blood flow, which assists with the natural blood clotting process. Proper direct pressure can even stop hemorrhage from carotid arteries—the arteries found in your neck—and femoral arteries—artery found inside your thighs. When applying direct pressure, do not release pressure to check the wound until you are prepared to control the bleeding by packing the wound or by applying a tourniquet. Utilize help from the patient or from others. The more hands, the better. Keep in mind that it's hard to use direct pressure to maintain control of big bleeders while moving the casualty. If possible, make sure a proper pressure dressing or a tourniquet is applied prior to moving the injured.

Trauma Kits

To better treat the wounded, we need to discuss what should go into a basic trauma kit. This is not a First Aid kit, so the OSHA approved Band-Aids and aspirin should not be in this kit. First, you should have Nitrile or exam gloves to protect those rendering medical help; these are inexpensive and multiple pairs should be included. Medical scissors or trauma shires should also be included, as they will assist in cutting of cloths to expose wounds.

No trauma kit should be without rolls (not squares) of Kerlex and compressed gauze, which are made of high-quality cotton for maximum absorption and stability. Gauze takes care of moderate to severe wounds involving heavy blood loss. Kerlex is specially designed for bandaging heads, limbs, and difficult-to-dress wounds. From my experience, both are invaluable and an absolute must have when treating wounds. This kit should also have Israeli or any other pressure dressing type of bandage. The Israeli bandage is an effective, multifunctional treatment for controlling traumatic bleeding. It is an all-in-one solution, which combines multiple first aid applications, including primary dressing, pressure applicator, secondary dressing, and foolproof closure apparatus to secure the bandage in place.

The SWAT-T (Stretch-Wrap-And-Tuck Tourniquet) is simple to use and needs to be applied when hemorrhaging is severe (arterial) and loss of life is immanent without stopping the bleeding. In most patients, tourniquets have been proven to be safe for the limb when left on for up to two hours. However, it is important to know that, even when used properly, tourniquets may cause loss of limb. Still, this is a necessary risk, especially when the outcome could be saving an individual's life.

The SWAT-T is a cost-effective multifunctional piece of medical equipment which is 1/3 the price of other single function tourniquets. Its primary role is of a tourniquet, but it can also be used as elastic bandage. You can use the SWAT-T to hold ice near sprains and strains, stabilize a twisted knee/ankle, or to sling a shoulder. The SWAT-T can also be used to loosely apply pressure across the chest or abdomen and can be used to splint an extremity to the body, other leg, or to a rigid object for immobilization.

There are many other advanced medical options that could go into a trauma bag; however, to keep it simple, there are only two other items that are recommended: chest seal and emergency blanket. A chest seal is used for treating open pneumothorax and preventing tension pneumothorax, also known as a sucking chest wound, which are the results of a gunshot, stab wounds, or other penetrating chest trauma. The emergency blanket is good to keep patients warm and reduce the chance of hypothermia.[5] Even in an office environment, or in the heat of the desert, if the individual has a large amount of blood loss, their body temperature will drop, thus running the risk of hypothermia. This individual kit that I just described can be put together cost effectively for around $45 each. It's important to have multiple individual kits around your organization in various locations so they are not just centrally located. If an event was to occur, the location will be random, and kits need to be available immediately.

This is not an all-inclusive list of medical equipment. There are tons of different medical equipment on the market and several person preferences. The only other possible addi-

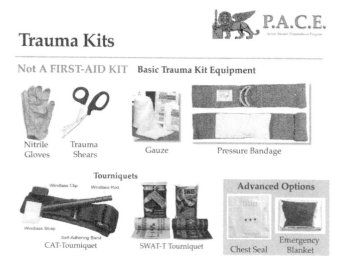

Trauma Kits   P.A.C.E.

Not A FIRST-AID KIT   Basic Trauma Kit Equipment

Nitrile Gloves   Trauma Shears   Gauze   Pressure Bandage

Tourniquets

CAT-Tourniquet   SWAT-T Tourniquet   Advanced Options   Chest Seal   Emergency Blanket

---

5 Hypothermia is a medical emergency that occurs when your body loses heat faster than it can produce heat.

tion I would add is the CAT Tourniquets, also called Combat application Tourniquets. These are extremely effective, but costly, and require limited training to put into action.

Alternatives to Professional Trauma Kits

Now that we discussed proper medical equipment, let's think outside the box in the event you don't have any of those items. What can be used as substitutes? For bandages, anything made of cotton will work. Using the patient's clothing or using your clothing to pack wounds and use as pressure bandages can and will work. Preferably, if you are rendering aid, use your clothing first to avoid the injured from potentially getting hypothermia. Try and stay away from nylon and polyester, as they won't absorb blood, so they won't help as much as cotton. Polyester and nylon can be used for slings and extra wadding for pressure dressing. However, if this is all you have, it's better than

P.A.C.E.

Trauma Kits - Alternatives

STOP THE BLEED

Use whatever you can, don't worry about how clean or sterile the material is.

Bandages
- Anything Cotton

- Nylon and polyester is good for pressure dressing material, but will not absorb fluid

- Female Hygiene products work but are limited in material

Tourniquets
- General Rule 2-3 fingers in width

Infections can be cured IF the patient is alive

nothing. Female hygiene products work great considering what their main purpose is. Keep in mind the actual cotton inside is limited and you may need to use multiples to be affective.

To create a tourniquet, the general rule is they should be two–three fingers in width; shoe laces will not work. The main principal of a tourniquet is to apply a wide width of pressure thus closing the end of the bleeding artery. Shoe laces will only cut into the flesh and not provide the pressure needed.

In the pictures you see a wide variety of possible medical equipment. Men's shirts, undershirts, and socks can be used as bandages, and possible tourniquets; ties, belts, and strap on the laptop bag could be used as a tourniquet. A woman's purse strap could be used as a tourniquet and so could her scarf—depending on the material, it could also be used as a bandage. There are many options that could be used if proper medical equipment isn't available. If you are in a dire situation, you must think outside the box to potentially save lives. Regardless of what you use, don't worry about how clean or sterile the material is. We have had tremendous advances in medicine and infections can be cured *if* the patient is alive.

Tourniquets

Tourniquets must be applied without delay for life threating bleeding. Remember the average time it takes a person to bleed to death is only two–four minutes; time is critical. They should be applied as high up on the limb as possible. The reason is because you don't know where the end of the artery is.

For example: Take a rubber band and stretch it out; that is your artery. If you cut that rubber band, it retracts and becomes a quarter of its stretched-out length. That is the same thing that happens when an artery is cut; it retracts and you won't know how far up that limb it has gone. If the tourniquet is placed below where the artery has retracted to, then the tourniquet is rendered ineffective and the injured will still bleed to death. Tighten the tourniquet until the bleeding has stopped—this should be self-explanatory of why it's important. Note the time of application; this is important information for the doctor who will ultimately remove the tourniquet. The length of time that the tourniquet has been in place will determine what steps the doctor needs to take prior to the removal of the tourniquet.

Periodically, check to make sure the bleeding hasn't restarted. There are several reasons why bleeding may restart: the tourniquet got bumped and loosened; it wasn't initially properly secured; after the initial trauma, swelling in the area has gone down thus making the tourniquet not as tight as it initially was.

You need to indicate on the injured that a tourniquet has been applied. Don't assume that medical professionals will be aware that the injured has a tourniquet on. The easiest way to accomplish this is to make a T on the patient's forehead, using the patient's own blood. It's a reality that if you need to put on a tourniquet there will be a lot of blood to use; this again reflects back to having the right mindset to accept the reality of the what the situation will be like.

SWAT-T Tourniquet Application

SWAT-T, or Stretch Wrap and Tuck Tourniquet, is a unique multi-purpose medical device. The wide elastic band construction of the SWAT-T has been clinically shown to function effectively at lower pressures than traditional windlass style tourniquets. This means less potential for injury to the patient and less pain from the tourniquet. The SWAT-T's unique design allows it to serve as a tourniquet, pressure dressing, and elastic wrap among numerous other potential uses.

The simple stretch, wrap, and tuck method is easily learned and retained by non-medical personnel and medical providers alike. The SWAT-T is compact, lightweight, and economical. The SWAT-T generally can be purchased for around $10 versus $30 for the other tourniquets on the market. The SWAT-T packaging has six tear points located on the sides of the package, allowing for traditional horizontal opening at the top, bottom, or center of the package.

Pressure indicator markings allow the SWAT-T to service both a tourniquet, a device that stops blood flow to a limb, and a pressure dressing, a device designed to cover a wound and apply pressure. There are markings located along the exterior of the SWAT-T to visually indicate the amount of pressure being applied and which mode the device is functioning in. The more the SWAT-T is stretched while wrapping around the limb, the more pressure it will apply; this will be indicated by the oval markings becoming circles and the diamonds in the center of the oval is becoming squares. Concurrently, the strip of rectangles above the ovals will become a strip of squares.

When the SWAT-T is used as a pressure dressing, it should be wrapped tightly enough to apply pressure to the wound, but not so tightly that the ovals diamonds and rectangle strips distort to the tourniquet pressure indicator shapes. When used as a tourniquet, the SWAT-T should be applied between the wound and the body, tightly enough to stop all blood flow to the limb. Be sure to overlap the first wrap of the tourniquet to secure it in place and subsequent wraps should be tight enough to stop blood flow as shown on the pressure indicator marking. On the final wrap, remember to place your fingers underneath the SWAT-T to provide a place to tuck the tail of the tourniquet in order to secure it in place. If you forget to do this, do not unwrap the tourniquet; rather, simply locate the edge of a previous wrap and pull it up to make room to securely tuck the tail underneath.

It will be difficult to wrap the tourniquet without some twisting or bunching in a real-world application. Nevertheless, every effort should be made to apply the SWAT-T as flat as possible, since less pressure is required to stop blood flow with a wider tourniquet, which are also safer and more comfortable for the patient. Never remove a functioning tourniquet simply to straighten a twisted or bunched up section. In the unlikely event that bleeding continues, a second SWAT-T can be applied above below or directly on top of the first SWAT-T

Ideally, you want to expose the limb and visually identify the source of bleeding. The acceptable location for any tourniquet is as high up on the limb as possible. Careful monitoring should be continued after tourniquet application to ensure that all bleeding is controlled. Always double check the tourniquet application after you move a patient.

You will not be able to apply a tourniquet to some wounds such as the neck, abdomen, armpit, or groin. These wounds should be treated by packing with a hemostatic agent or gauze and then utilizing the SWAT –T as pressure dressing. The purpose of the SWAT-T, in this instance, is to apply pressure to the packing material and to protect the wound from further contamination. Be aware of how tight you wrap the SWAT-T in this application and check the pressure indicator-markings making sure it is not so tight where it has turned into a tourniquet.

The tourniquet application band is a patient information device located in the center of the rolled SWAT-T, which can be applied to the patient's wrist once bleeding is controlled. You may fill in appropriate patient care information such as patient name, tourniquet application time, heart rate, blood pressure, blood type, and whether a radial pulse is present. If time does not permit to fill this out, simply mark the patients forehead with a T to indicate a tourniquet has been applied. This can be done with a marker, lipstick, or using the patient's own blood.

CAT (Combat Application Tourniquet)

The CAT Tourniquet is what is most often utilized by military and law enforcement. It is small light weight and can easily be applied using one. This allows the injured to be able to easily apply the tourniquet to their own injury. Unlike the SWAT-T, this tourniquet cannot be used as a pressure dressing; it has one purpose only, to be applied as a tourniquet.

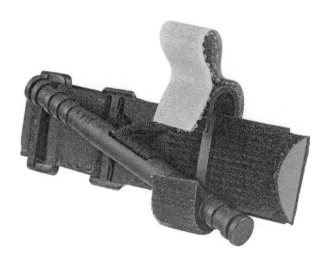

Components of the CAT Tourniquet

Steps to apply the CAT according to Bleeding Control (BCON) Basic training[6]

- Step 1: Open up the tourniquet and insert the wounded extremity (arm or leg) through the loop of the C-A-T™
- Step 2: Pull the free end of the self-adhering band as tight as you possibly can and fasten it back on itself

6 Bleeding Control Website www.bleedingcontrol.org

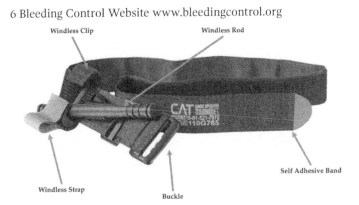

- It is important that you remove all the slack out of the tourniquet in order for the tourniquet to function properly
- Step 3: Wrap the free end of the strap around the extremity and adhere the band to itself
- Wrap it up to the clip on the tourniquet but don't go past the clip
- Step 4: Twist the windlass rod until the bleeding has stopped
- If you pulled it as tight as you could earlier in step 2 and removed all of the slack out of the tourniquet, it will take you no more than two to three 180 degree turns of the windlass to make it tight and stop bleeding
- If it is taking more turns than that, you probably did not remove enough of the slack when first pulling it tight
- Step 5: Lock the windlass rod in place by inserting it into the windlass clip
- The victim's bleeding from that extremity should now be stopped
- Step 6: Adhere the remainder of the long self-adhering strap over the windlass rod and place it through the windlass clip
- Continue to adhere it to itself around the extremity as far as it will go
- Step 7: Secure the rod and the band in place with the small windlass strap, which will usually be either white or gray in color and has the word "time" written on it
- Grasp the end of the windlass strap, pull it tight over the windlass clip, and adhere it to the opposite side hook on the windlass clip
- This will prevent the windlass from becoming dislodged when the victim is moved for transport

- Step 8: Finally, note the time that the tourniquet was applied
- If you have a marker or pen, you can write the time directly on the windlass strap of the tourniquet
- If you don't have something you can use to write the time, you should still note the time that is was applied and then, when the medical responders arrive, verbally tell them what time you placed the tourniquet

Wound Packing

First, locate and examine the wound, and identify the point of bleeding. Then, remove excess pooled blood from the wound, while preserving any clots already in the wound, if possible. Next, pack the wound with gauze, or other cotton material directly in and over the source of bleeding. Ensure you have good initial contact; use as much gauze as needed to stem the blood flow.

Continue to pack entire dressing while maintaining good contact. The remainder of gauze can be applied on top of the wound or to wrap the wound depending on location. Quickly apply pressure until bleeding has stopped—two to three minutes of continuous pressure is suggested. Leave gauze in place and wrap to secure it in and over the wound. Periodically check the placement of dressing ensuring it has not shifted and it is still properly placed over the wound. Make sure that there is no active bleeding from the edges but do not lift dressing to reassess.

Occasionally, the bandage will become soaked as it will be due to active uncontrolled bleeding. In this case, entirely remove the old gauze and replace it with a new one following the same steps; utilize the pressure bandage or an elastic bandage such as the SWAT tourniquet. If you are using any type of hemostatic gauze, make sure the empty gauze package containing removal instructions is sent with the patient to the hospital.

This illustration shows the difference between packing the wound or just allowing blood to pool in the wound. Remember that pressure stops the bleeding, so the more pressure we apply, the sooner the patient stops bleeding and the higher probably they have of survival.

To properly pack a wound start by stuffing your material into the wound; continue to do so using as many fingers as necessary. This will not be comfortable for the patient but you are trying to save their life. Once you have packed the wound until you can no longer pack any more material into the wound, immediately apply pressure.

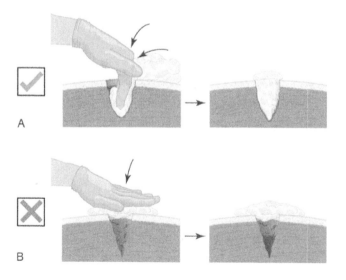

CPR

During crisis situations it is recommended that CPR *not to be performed.* If cardiac arrest is caused due to a significant event or a trauma, the patient stays dead. Because CPR cannot be stopped once started, unless properly relieved, the hard choice should be made to instead focus on those that can be saved.

Hemostatic Dressings

There is medical gauze on the market that helps promote clotting for severe injuries. This gauze is impregnated with a hemostatic agent or granular hemostatic agents to help clotting, thus stopping the bleed. This opens up the question: What is better, a roll of regular gauze, or this new hemostatic gauze? If we understand that what ultimately stops the bleeding is pressure, then I would argue that a roll of gauze is just as effective as a hemostatic dressing. Again, I have used both on real wounded casualties and, personally, a roll of gauze is easier to use and just as effective.

It would appear my observation has also been the subject of studies done by various groups of medical doctors. In fact, "Standard gauze dressing was as efficacious as Celox-A, Chitoflex, and combat gauze in treating uncontrolled hemorrhage from small penetrating wounds not amenable to tourniquet placement. The present findings also suggest that the form factor of poured granules may not be as effective as tube-delivered hemostatic granules or gauze products."[7]

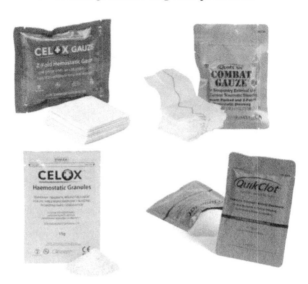

Although great advances have been made as it pertains to hemostatic agents, there are also multiple side effects and detractors that need to be addressed and considered.

- According to published data gained from both animal studies and case reports, the thermal injury and burns resulting from the exothermic reaction and the poor biodegradability are the main challenges for QuikClot. However, although it is claimed that the use of QuikClot ACS+, unlike the previous generation, does not cause thermal injury, there are currently no large-scale clini-

---

7 Lanny F. Littlejohn MD at al. "Comparison of Celox-A, ChitoFlex, WoundStat, and Combat Gauze Hemostatic Agents Versus Standard Gauze Dressing in Control of Hemorrhage in a Swine Model of Penetrating Trauma," Journal of the Society for Academic Emergency Medicine 18, no. 4 (April 2011): 340–350.

cal reports regarding the occurrence of such a complication after the application of the QuikClot ACS+ on the wound.

- It is worrisome that all the hemostatic agents composed of granules can leave residue in the interior of the blood vessels. In addition, all of these agents may obstruct arterial flow. Those hemostats that activate the clotting pathway can also cause distal thrombosis.
- Significant blood loss leads to hypothermia and hemostatic agents can fail if and when the patient is experiencing hypothermia.
- A basic single bandage of a hemostatic agents generally starts at $40; however, a roll of gauze starts at $1.
- Expiration dates for standard gauze far surpass the one–three year life span of hemostatic dressings.

It should be noted that any of the above-mentioned agents can fail if applied incorrectly; therefore, appropriate training is the key to minimizing this risk.

In summary, QuickClot and other hemostatic dressings look and sound fantastic, but what real advantages do they provide? I am not saying that hemostatic agents do not work; rather, I am saying that understanding how they work and their side effects should be considered. I would rather put the money towards increasing additional medical supplies and getting more bang for the buck.

Force Multiplier

Now that you have a basic understanding of some medical treatments that can be applied to save lives, you are a force multiplier, a factor that dramatically increases the effectiveness of a process or system. Basically, you can now spread your knowledge to others. How can this help in an Active Assailant situation?

First, it can provide you with assistance. If you are involved in an incident, you can direct others as to what they need to do to assist you. By assigning duties to others, you shift focus off the situation and give them task and purpose. This can help those that are in complete shock of the situation, so instead of thinking about what just happened, they shift their focus to the instructions you are giving to them and the tasks you have asked them to do. These can be simple tasks, such as to find more medical supplies or asking them to hold pressure on a wound. This also applies to giving task and purpose to those who are injured. Now, instead of you looking for medical supplies or applying pressure to an injury, you have someone else doing it, freeing you up to help others. Ultimately, this can save lives because the more hands involved, the quicker the bleeding is tended to and hopefully stopped. One thing is guaranteed uncontrolled bleeding has a 100% fatality rate, if not treated. Remember: direction pressure, tourniquet, and reassess.

Evacuate

Never, never, never give up.
– Winston Churchill

There are some important considerations you must think about before evacuating an Active Assailant scene. We have already discussed issues like having an escape route and knowing where the exits are, but here are a few other considerations.

Do you know how many Active Assailants are there? In the situation at Columbine High School, there were two assailants and they were not always together; they moved around attacking people in different locations. First responders do not know who the Active Assailant is or how many

99

there are. For all they know, you could be an Active Assailant wanting to do them harm, and you can imagine what could happen then.

There might be other potential hazards, such as boobie traps, pipe bombs, etc. Active Assailants continue to add to their arsenal and may not simply rely on one weapon to use to cause harm and death. You may not be mentally prepared for the visual truth, aftermath, and results of the Active Assailant.

Before you evacuate, consider the option of staying right where you are. If you have followed the other recommendations in the P.A.C.E. program, then you have successfully put multiple barriers between you and the attacker and are relatively safe. Remember attackers are going to go the path of least resistance to do as much damage as possible. If they can't get to you, they move on to those they can get to, unless you are the target. If you stay in your location, the emergency response team will find you once the scene is clear and safe. They won't leave you behind.

Once you have decided to evacuate, do not attempt to move any wounded people. Remember your commitment is to the action of evacuating; if you stop to move the wounded, you are creating the opportunity for you to become a victim as well. Leave your belongings behind. Once outside, you should help prevent others from entering an area where the Active Assailant might be.

Follow any and all instructions given to you by law enforcement. Remember they don't know who you are. They have the responsibility to ensure everyone's safety so if they tell you to lay flat on the ground, that's for your protection and for their as well, so there is no need to argue. Call 911 when you are safe; this can help with accountability during and after an incident.

Information for 911

It may see pretty simple, but under stress it will be difficult to focus on information that you will need to provide to 911. Some basic information that you should provide to 911 includes:

- Name and location of your building and your personal location
- Location of the Active Assailant(s)
- Number of assailants, if known
- Physical description of assailant(s)
- Number and type of weapons held by the assailant(s)
- Number of potential victims at your location

When Law Enforcement Arrives

When law enforcement arrives, it's important that a few things are understood. One thing that people forget about is that first responders are human and they are nervous, scared, and under stress as well. As scared as you are, you aren't tasked to hunt down the attacker. They selflessly go in not knowing how many attackers there are, and what types of weapons they may have, or how skilled they may be.

Their purpose is to stop the killing as quickly as possible. They will proceed directly to the last area in which shots were reported to be fired. As discussed in the Care section, their initial response is not to tend to the wounded. Officers may shout commands and may push individuals to the ground for their safety. Remember, law enforcement don't know who you are so, to them, everyone is a suspect.

Flash grenades, tear gas, and pepper spray may be utilized to stun and hinder the attacker; if you are in close proximity you may also be affected. Officers usually arrive in teams of two or four; however, depending on the police department standard operating procedure, it may require more or less to arrive before they make entry. Officers may be wearing civilian clothes, regular patrol uniforms, external bullet proof vests, Kevlar Helmets, or other tactical equipment. They may be armed with handguns, rifles, or shotguns. This is all helpful information in getting in the right mindset of knowing what to expect.

Active Assailant, Workplace Violence, and other emergency situations are happening more often and are unpredictable. Consider the possibilities of not being prepared. It is up to us to control as much as we can. We can't control or stop crazy, but we can control our mindset and our preparation.

Remember:
- Prepare
- Action
- Care
- Evacuate

Being prepared starts with having the right mindset to realize that there is always the potential for a significant emotional event. **Don't be paranoid. Be prepared. It could save your life.**

Glossary

A

Access Control
In the fields of physical security and information security, access control (AC) is the selective restriction of access to a place or other resource.

Active Assailant
An Active Assailant(s) means a person or group of persons actively engaged in killing or attempting to kill or cause serious bodily injury to a person or group of persons.

Active Assailant Policy and Procedure
Policies and procedures that are designed to influence and determine all major decisions and actions, and all activities take place within the boundaries set by them. Procedures are the specific methods employed to express policies in action in day-to-day operations of the organization.

Active Shooter
An Active Shooter is an individual actively engaged in killing or attempting to kill people in a confined and populated area; in most cases, active shooters use firearms(s) and there is no pattern or method to their selection of victims.

Alert
Warn (someone) of a danger, threat, or problem, typically with the intention of having it avoided or dealt with.

B

Background Checks

A background check or background investigation is the process of looking up and compiling criminal records, commercial records, and financial records of an individual or an organization.

Barrier

An obstacle that prevents movement or access

Behavior

The way in which one acts or conducts oneself, especially toward others.

Bleeding

To lose blood from the vascular system, either internally into the body or externally through a natural orifice or break in the skin

Bleeding Control (BCON)

BCON is a course developed, organized and trained by BleedingControl.org, an initiative of the ACS and the Hartford Consensus, aims to provide the public with proper bleeding control techniques. More information can be found at www.bleedingcontrol.org

Body Language

The process of communicating nonverbally through conscious or unconscious gestures and movements.

Boston Bombing Incident

During the annual Boston Marathon on April 15, 2013, two homemade bombs detonated 12 seconds and 210 yards (190 m) apart at 2:49 p.m., near the finish line of the race, killing three people and injuring several hundred others, including 16 who lost limbs.

Buddy Aid

The act of assisting the wounded in order to treat wounds and save life.

Bullying

Abuse and mistreatment of someone vulnerable by someone stronger, more powerful. Bullying is unwanted, aggressive, intimidation, emotional mistreatment behavior among individuals that involves a real or perceived power imbalance. The behavior is repeated, or has the potential to be repeated, over time.

C

Columbine High School Active Shooter

The Columbine High School massacre was a school shooting that occurred on April 20, 1999, at Columbine High School in Columbine, an unincorporated area of Jefferson County, Colorado, United States, in the Denver metropolitan area. In addition to the shootings, the complex and highly planned attack involved a fire bomb to divert firefighters, propane tanks converted to bombs placed in the cafeteria, 99 explosive devices, and car bombs. The perpetrators, senior students Eric Harris and Dylan Klebold, murdered 12 students and one teacher.

They injured 21 additional people, and three more were injured while attempting to escape the school. After exchanging gunfire with responding police officers, the pair subsequently committed suicide.

Compression
Applying direct pressure to an open wound in the effort to stop the victim from bleeding.

CPR
Short for cardiopulmonary resuscitation. An emergency procedure in which the heart and lungs are made to work by compressing the chest overlying the heart and forcing air into the lungs. CPR is used to maintain circulation when the heart has stopped pumping on its own.

CPTED
Crime Prevention Through Environmental Design (CPTED) is defined as a multi-disciplinary approach to deterring criminal behavior through environmental design. CPTED strategies rely upon the ability to influence offender decisions that precede criminal acts by affecting the built, social and administrative environment.

Crisis Management Plan
A crisis management plan (CMP) is a document that outlines the processes an organization will use to respond to a critical situation that would negatively affect its profitability, reputation or ability to operate.

D

Dabiq Magazine

Dabiq is an online magazine used by the Islamic State of Iraq and the Levant (ISIL) for Islamic radicalization and recruitment. It was first published in July 2014 in a number of different languages including English.

De-escalation

Behavior that is intended to escape escalations of conflicts. It may also refer to approaches in conflict resolution

DHS

The United States Department of Homeland Security (DHS) is a federal agency designed to protect the United States against threats. Its wide-ranging duties include aviation security, border control, emergency response and cybersecurity.

Direct Pressure

Applying force to an open wound in the effort to stop the victim from bleeding.

E

EMS

The acronym for Emergency Medical Services. This term refers to the treatment and transport of people in crisis health situations that may be life threatening. Emergency medical support is applied in a wide variety of situations

Extremity
A limb or appendage. The arm may be identified by the layperson as an upper extremity and the leg as a lower extremity.

F

Facility Security Measures
Physical security describes security measures that are designed to deny unauthorized access to facilities, equipment and resources and to protect personnel and property from damage or harm (such as espionage, theft, or terrorist attacks).

Fatality
A death caused by an accident or by violence, or a person who has died in this way

FBI
The FBI is a government agency in the United States that investigates crimes in which a national law is broken or in which the country's security is threatened. FBI is an abbreviation for 'Federal Bureau of Investigation.'

Fight
Take part in a violent struggle involving the exchange of physical blows or the use of weapons.

First Responder
A person (such as a police officer or an EMT) who is among those responsible for going immediately to the scene of an accident or emergency to provide assistance.

Force Multiplier

A factor or a combination of factors that dramatically increases (hence "multiplies") the effectiveness of an item or group, giving a given number of individuals or weapons (or other hardware) the ability to accomplish greater things than without it.

G

Gauze

Originally made of silk and was used for clothing. It is now used for many different things, including gauze sponges for medical purposes. When used as a medical dressing, gauze is generally made of cotton. It is especially useful for dressing wounds where other fabrics might stick to the burn or laceration.

H

Hemorrhage

A copious or heavy discharge of blood from the blood vessels

Hide

Put or keep out of sight; conceal from the view or notice of others.

Hot Zone

An area that is considered to be dangerous. It generally entails special equipment to protect those who enter the area

I

Incident Responses Teams
An incident response team or emergency response team (ERT) is a group of people who prepare for and respond to any emergency incident, such as a natural disaster or an interruption of business operations. Incident response teams are common in public service organizations as well as in organizations.

Inspire Magazine
Inspire is an English language online magazine reported to be published by the organization al-Qaeda in the Arabian Peninsula (AQAP). The magazine is one of the many ways AQAP uses the Internet to reach its audience.

Israeli Bandage
The Israeli bandage is an innovative, combat proven first-aid device for the staunching of blood flow from traumatic hemorrhage wounds in pre-hospital emergency situations.

J

Junctional Area
Portions of the body including neck, shoulder and groin area

K

L

Lockdown
To make people stay in a locked indoor space during an emergency in order to keep them safe

M

Mass Casualty Incident
Any incident in which emergency medical services resources, such as personnel and equipment, are overwhelmed by the number and severity of casualties.

Medic Aid
Professional medical treatment administered by trained medical professionals

Mindset
A fixed mental attitude or disposition that predetermines a person's responses to and interpretations of situations.

Motivation
The reason or reasons one has for acting or behaving in a particular way.

Mutual Support Agreement
A written agreement between agencies, organizations, or jurisdictions to lend assistance across jurisdictional boundaries. It agrees to assist by furnishing personnel, equipment, and expertise in a specified manner at requisite time.

N

National Association of Emergency Medical Technicians NAEMT
Formed in 1975 and more than 65,000 members strong, the National Association of Emergency Medical Technicians (NAEMT) is the nation's only organization that represents and serves the professional interests of all EMS practitioners, including paramedics, emergency medical technicians, emergency medical responders, and other professionals providing prehospital and out-of-hospital emergent, urgent or preventive medical care.

Nitrile Gloves
Nitrile gloves are made out of a synthetic rubber, and are an ideal alternative when latex allergies are of concern. Nitrile gloves are the superior glove when it comes to puncture resistance. Nitrile gloves are often referred to as "medical grade."

Nonverbal Ques
Nonverbal communication involves the conscious and unconscious processes of encoding and decoding. Encoding is the act of generating information such as facial expressions, gestures, and postures.

O

OODA Loop
The OODA loop is the decision cycle of observe, orient, decide, and act

OSHA

OSHA: The Occupational Safety and Health Administration, an agency of the US government under the Department of Labor with the responsibility of ensuring safety at work and a healthful work environment. OSHA's mission is to prevent work-related injuries, illnesses and deaths.

P

Paramedic

A healthcare professional who responds to medical emergencies outside of a hospital. Paramedics mainly work as part of emergency medical services (EMS), most often in ambulances. The scope of practice of a paramedic varies among countries, but generally includes autonomous decision making around the emergency care of patients.

Pathway to Violence

The prevailing theoretical model with regard to the assessment and management of targeted violence begins with the concept of a "pathway" to violence.

First mentioned by Dietz and Martell (1989) and systematically studied by Fein and Vossekuil (1998; 1999), behavioral pathway refers to the path along which an individual might progress in moving from communication with the target to approach.

The U.S. Secret Service developed a pathway model based on their empirical research describing a route moving from ideation, to planning, to preparation and finally to implementation.

Policy

A policy is a set of ideas or plans that is used as a basis for making decisions, especially in politics, economics, or business.

Prepare

To make ready beforehand for some purpose, use, or activity

Pressure Dressing

A bandage or cloth material firmly applied to exert pressure to stop bleeding

Procedure

The act, method, or manner of proceeding in some action; esp., the sequence of steps to be followed

Q

R

Rescue Task Force

The concept of the Rescue Task Force (RTF) came from the Arlington County (Virginia) Fire Department. ... Known as "warm zone integration," the RTF concept uses the phrase "Task Force," which is an ICS term for a unit consisting of mixed resources assembled to meet a specific tactical need.

Risk Assessments

A systematic process of evaluating the potential risks that may be involved in a projected activity or undertaking.

Risk Management Plans
A risk management plan is a document that a project manager prepares to foresee risks, estimate impacts, and define responses to issues. It also contains a risk assessment matrix. A risk is "an uncertain event or condition that, if it occurs, has a positive or negative effect on a project's objectives."

Rumiyah Magazine
Rumiyah was an online magazine used by the Islamic State of Iraq and the Levant for propaganda and recruitment. It was first published in September 2016 and is released in several languages, including English, French, German, Russian, Indonesian and Uyghur.

Run
Move at a speed faster than a walk, never having both or all the feet on the ground at the same time.

S

Self-Aid
Process of caring for your own wounds

Situational Awareness
The perception of environmental elements and events with respect to time or space, the comprehension of their meaning, and the projection of their future status.

Sounds – During an Incident
Vibrations that travel through the air or another medium and can be heard when they reach a person's or animal's ear.

Stressor
A stimulus that causes stress

Suspicious Activity
Suspicious activity is any observed behavior that could indicate terrorism or terrorism-related crime

Suspicious Bags or Packages
Bags or Packages left unattended and or unclaimed.

Swarm Attack
Offensive tactic to gather as many persons to attack and overwhelm a intended target

T

Table Top Exercise
An activity in which key personnel assigned emergency management roles and responsibilities are gathered to discuss, in a non-threatening environment, various simulated emergency situations.

Tactical Combat Casualty Care (TCCC)
Tactical Combat Casualty Care is the standard of care in Prehospital Battlefield Medicine. The TCCC Guidelines are routinely updated and published by the Committee on Tactical Combat Casualty Care, a component of the Joint Trauma System. TCCC was designed in the mid-'90s for the Special Operations medical community.

Tactical Emergency Casualty Care (TECC)
NAEMT's Tactical Emergency Casualty Care (TECC) teaches EMS practitioners and other prehospital providers how to respond to and care for patients in a civilian tactical environment. It is designed to decrease preventable deaths in a tactical situation.

Tension pneumothorax
A wound in the chest wall which acts as a valve that permits air to enter the pleural cavity but prevents its escape.

The X
The specific location of a incident or attack.

Tourniquet
A device for stopping the flow of blood through a vein or artery, typically by compressing a limb with a cord or tight bandage.

Tourniquet (CAT)
Combat Application Tourniquet utilizes a durable windlass system with a patented free-moving internal band providing true circumferential pressure to the extremity. Once adequately tightened, bleeding will cease and the windlass is locked into place. A hook and loop windlass retention strap is then applied, securing the windlass to maintain pressure during casualty evacuation. The C-A-T®'s unique dual securing system avoids the use of screws and clips which can become difficult to operate under survival stress or where fine motor skills are compromised.

Tourniquet (SWAT-T)

The SWAT-Tourniquet is a unique and multipurpose dressing. ... The SWAT-Tourniquet is made of elastic material which allows a more rapid means to control extremity bleeding and allows application higher into the groin and axilla than other tourniquets.

Training

The process by which someone is taught the skills that are needed to perform certain tasks

Trauma Kit

A medical kit containing supplies useful for controlling bleeding and injuries in emergencies.

U

V

Verbal Queues

Perceptual information communicated in a social exchange by signs accompanying the words used in speech

Vulnerability Assessments

A vulnerability assessment is the process of identifying, quantifying, and prioritizing the vulnerabilities in a system.

W

Warning Signs
A type of sign which indicates a potential hazard, obstacle or condition requiring special attention

Weapon
A thing designed or used for inflicting bodily harm or physical damage.

Workplace Violence
Any act or threat of physical violence, harassment, intimidation, or other threatening disruptive behavior that occurs at the work site. It ranges from threats and verbal abuse to physical assaults and even homicide. It can affect and involve employees, clients, customers and visitors.

Workplace Violence Plan
A comprehensive plan in place that identifies and offers ways to reduce risks, provides means for employees to raise concerns and report issues, communicates and reinforces emergency procedures, and establishes procedures to track progress over time.

Wounded
Serious injury, especially a deep cut through the skin.

X

Y

Z

.

References

- https://www.dictionary.com
- https://en.wikipedia.org/wiki/Main_Page
- https://www.bleedingcontrol.org
- https://www.fbi.gov
- https://www.asisonline.org
- Department of Homeland "Security Active Shooter How to Respond". http://www.dhs.gov
- Department Justice Federal Bureau of Investigation "A Study of Active Shooter Incidents in the United States Between 2000 and 2103" http://www.fbi.gov
- United States Secret Service – National Threat Assessment Center Mass Attacks in Public Spaces -2017 https://www.secretservice.gov/forms/USSS_NTAC-Mass_Attacks_in_Public_Spaces-2017.pdf
- https://medical-dictionary.thefreedictionary.com
- https://www.merriam-webster.com/dictionary/
- https://www.osha.gov
- https://www.nbcnews.com/storyline/vegas-cop-killers/cost-bravery-vegas-bystander-died-trying-stop-rampage-n127361